Beginning

Drama
4–11

Second Edition

Joe Winston and Miles Tandy

David Fulton Publishers
London

Contents

David Fulton Publishers Ltd
414 Chiswick High Road
London W4 5TF

www.fultonpublishers.co.uk

First published in Great Britain by David Fulton Publishers 1998
Reprinted 1999 (twice)
Second edition published 2001
Reprinted 2001, 2002, 2003
10 9 8 7 6 5 4

Note: The right of Joe Winston and Miles Tandy to be identified as the authors of this work has been asserted by them in accordance with the Copyright, Designs and Patents Act 1988.

British Library Cataloguing in Publication Data
A catalogue record for this book is available from the British Library

ISBN 1–85346–702–2

Typeset by FiSH Books, London
Printed and bound in Scotland by Scotprint, Haddington

Introduction

Ask a group of primary school teachers or student teachers what the word *drama* suggests to them and you are likely to receive a mixture of responses. Many will reply with words such as role-play, improvisation, speaking and listening, imagination, creativity, self-expression. Some – but only some – will mention performance, acting, plays. A few will mention the word fun, but a substantial minority will reply with words such as embarrassment, fear, or even terror. With a little prodding, these anxieties can be seen to relate either to their experiences as children at the hands of insensitive teachers or to their current anxieties as actual or potential teachers of drama. They often centre around issues of control and around the worry that teachers sometimes have that they lack the extrovert qualities and personal dynamism they feel that drama demands. They can also reflect a deeper misgiving, a vagueness as to what drama in the primary school is actually supposed to be about and what its inclusion in the curriculum entails.

In contrast, many children who have had little or no experience of drama in schools but who have come across the term in their everyday lives are quite clear that it is about plays and play-acting, about TV and film, and that dramas tell stories. The contrast in responses is an interesting one for, whereas those of the children reflect a cultural understanding of drama which is broadly shared in our society, those of the teachers recognise that, in schools, drama has come to mean something rather different, with its own vocabulary and its own frames of reference. This book begins with the premise that such a categorical distinction is unnecessary and unhelpful because it hides from teachers the fact that both they and their children know a lot more about drama than they often realise.

There has never been such a cultural saturation of drama in western society as there is today. Live theatres may be struggling but a brief scan through the TV journals will reveal that dramas of all sorts dominate the channels. Soaps, hospital and historical dramas, thrillers and police dramas, sitcoms and science fiction, all constitute the hard core of programming meant to attract and hold audiences counted in millions. Then there is the huge market for films, whether on TV, video or in the cinema. News programmes and documentaries often use dramatic formats to present information and advertisements use highly efficient mini-dramas to sell us a whole way of life. As individuals we may differ in our tastes and preferences, of course, and consequently in what we choose to watch, but there is little doubt that most of us today, adults and children, receive most of our stories in dramatic form.

The reason why so many teachers feel that they do not understand drama, or feel that what understanding they do have is partial and confused, is because much of this understanding is tacit; that is to say, they have acquired it without learning how to articulate it. This state of affairs is not helped by much of the language used to explain educational drama. Words such as performance, actor, scene, dialogue and audience are often absent from its discourse, to be replaced by a new set of concepts such as role-play, improvisation, hot-seating, teacher in role and still imaging. Making the leap from one discourse to the other can be confusing for the non-specialist or the novice drama teacher, as it does not help them relate their cultural understanding of drama to its practice in the classroom. Although there is a need for specialist terminology in educational drama, there is no need simultaneously to reject the language and ideas we use to describe the drama we experience in our wider cultural surroundings; an appreciation of the connections between the two will help inexperienced teachers get started and gain the confidence to continue teaching drama as part of their curriculum.

So what are some of the underlying principles of drama in its broader, cultural meaning and how can they inform its practice in primary classrooms?

1. Drama is playful

In one episode of *Blackadder*, Edmund, the Prince Regent's butler, bemoans the fact that he has to take Prince George to the theatre. George, it appears, thinks that everything that happens on stage is real. The previous week during a performance of *Julius Caesar*, just as Cassius was about to plunge in the knife, he had called out 'Look behind you, Mr Caesar'. Sure enough, we see him later that evening calling for the arrest of one of the actors for having committed 'murder' on stage. After Edmund has painstakingly explained once again that it's all only a play, a fact borne out when the murdered actor arises and waits for the Prince's applause, a *real* revolutionary terrorist suddenly jumps on to the stage and throws a *real* bomb on to George's lap. George applauds this exciting new turn in the play. 'It isn't a play any more, sir,' we hear Edmund call from behind the royal box, 'Put the bomb down and leave the theatre now.' George just has time to pooh-pooh Edmund for not being able to understand that it is, after all, only a play when the bomb explodes in his face.

Things that happen in drama are playful. People get angry but nobody really gets angry; people die but nobody really dies. The humour of the above extract hinges upon the fact that we take this understanding so much for granted that we find it hilarious that someone should be unable to make such a basic distinction. Since we were very young children, we have learned to distinguish between the conventions of play and those of everyday life and exploring the boundaries between the two can be a great source of delight for young children. This innate sense of playfulness persists as children grow and can be witnessed in the imaginative play areas in nursery or infant classrooms where, for example, a four-year-old boy might be seen to arrange some chairs into a line, call it his bus, take on the role of the bus driver, cast other children in role as his passengers and proceed to drive them all to London without ever actually moving the chairs. The apparent spontaneity of such play becomes shaped by the cultural environments within which children live, being channelled into a number of sporting or other cultural activities, of which various forms of drama can be among the most pervasive and significant. Drama and play are not, in the end, one and the same thing; but it is from children's innate capacity for play, and upon the understandings they gain from participating in play, that dramatic activity can be constructed.

2. Dramas use stories to explore issues of human significance

If human beings are essentially playful creatures then they are just as profoundly storytellers in the way they think and communicate experience. We communicate our daily experience to ourselves and to others in story form, we make sense of the behaviour of others by inventing stories to explain why they act as they do. Since prehistoric times, people have invented and told one another fictional stories and the practice persists today in jokes and comic books as well as in novels. Drama is a cultural activity which brings together these two human propensities for play and for storytelling. Play can be fun and stories can be entertaining but it is wrong to conclude that both activities are therefore trivial. The opposite of play is not work, nor is truth the opposite of story. On the contrary, it is through achieving the distance afforded by fiction that we can reflect more securely upon issues which have significant effects upon our daily lives.

3. In drama, the normal rules of time, place and identity are suspended

Dramatic time is elastic. A drama may last for an hour in real time but several months may pass in dramatic time. Whereas our daily lives are locked into the present, drama can leap back into the past or forward into the future and into numerous and varied places, some of which may never have existed. In these places and times, actors perform different identities, pretending to be other than they are, and these actions are witnessed by others, whether fellow actors or audience. The dramatic space itself needs to be clearly defined, to separate it from everyday reality and to mark where these transformations of time, place and identity are happening. Cinema and TV screens constitute such a space, fixed and permanent, where there is always the potential for drama to happen. In live drama, this space may be similarly permanent, such as a stage in a theatre. In a nursery or an infants' classroom, such a permanent space may be found in a well-planned, well-resourced imaginative play area or home corner.

The example of the boy and his imaginary bus is an interesting one to pursue further to illustrate how, through play, children learn to manipulate the core elements of drama. First of all, the boy appropriates the play space and transforms it into a dramatic space by building an imaginary bus. Objects in this space can, therefore, be given symbolic value; in other words, just as he can change his own identity and become a bus driver, chairs can represent something other than their everyday function. In the role of bus driver, the boy acts appropriately – steering and stopping the bus, asking for fares, getting under the chairs to repair the bus should it break down. His play has content, being about his experiences as a bus driver, and real time is suspended as this content is developed. The boy, despite the breakdown, drives to London and returns to the bus station in a matter of a few minutes.

Because dramatic time is only ever temporary, spaces for drama need not be permanent. In street theatre, for example, they may consist of no more than a section of pavement in the middle of a high street. In such cases, however, special efforts need to be taken to signal to those drawn into the spectacle that this *public* space has been transformed, for a short period, into a *dramatic* space. For most children in primary schools, drama takes place in a similarly shared public space, namely the school hall, and if teachers wish to engage children in worthwhile drama activities, they need to develop strategies which signal the transformation of this space into one where drama is able to happen.

4. Drama is a social activity and a communal art form

A common mistake is to consider the playwright as the sole creator of a drama, which subsequently exists as a written script. In its creation and in its reception, drama is a communal experience, shaped and shared by individuals working or watching in groups. A drama only becomes a drama when it is performed. In addition to the functions of the playwright, there are those of the director, the set designer, the lighting technician and the performers, who may include musicians as well as actors. In the case of a film or TV drama, the extensive length of the final credits is testimony to the communal resources that can be required to make drama happen. Audiences, too, are communal in nature. Even if I watch a TV drama alone in my lounge, I know that there are many others in my neighbourhood or circle of friends who are watching it too, and with whom I might talk about it later.

Classroom drama is a similarly social and communal experience but is more fluid and participatory in its form than most forms of theatre. The creative roles may be less rigidly defined and children will often take on at one and the same time the functions of playwright, director and actor, fashioning a text which may remain unscripted and be performed only once. The teacher, too, is part of this experience and can move in and out of particular functions, encouraging children to share actively in the shaping of a drama and in the witnessing of it. Just as the roles of actor and director may become blurred and coexist simultaneously in one child, the roles of actor and audience can interchange several times within the one lesson.

5. Drama is driven by rules and conventions

For a community to experience drama, individuals must first of all agree to submit to the dramatic event. In the case of TV drama, I switch on the set at the right time, sit down and ask not to be disturbed. In the case of most live drama, I buy a ticket, go to the theatre and contract into a number of social rules which will allow the drama to unfold. In most conventional theatres, I need to remain seated and silent, so as not to disturb either the performers or the audience. In this way, I respect both the drama and the intentions of the group of which I am a part. This is far from being a passive experience. I must watch, listen, concentrate, open myself to the play of thought and emotion that engagement with the drama promises, otherwise it will mean nothing to me. Essentially, I am agreeing to *actively participate* and some forms of drama demand more active participation than others – pantomimes, for example, where my vocal participation will be called for, or promenade theatre, where I must physically move in space in order to follow the action.

All social events need rules to guide them. These rules can be made explicit, as is the case in most classrooms, or they may be implicit, tacitly agreed and understood by those participating in the event. For classroom drama to succeed, teachers and children need to be clear about what the rules actually are and they must agree to follow them. Such rules are not restrictive or oppressive; they provide the framework within which groups can pursue common purposes. Any flouting of the rules disrupts these purposes and must be addressed. Classroom drama demands a wide range of behaviour patterns from children, ranging from high energy action, to talk, to stillness and attentive silence, each appropriate to different tasks. Its success will depend upon the children knowing what is expected of them and appreciating the rewards that come from doing it well, the rewards inherent to the experience of genuine engagement in a dramatic event.

6. Dramas should not be boring

Boredom is the cardinal sin as far as drama is concerned and it is the structure of a drama as much as its subject matter which keeps audiences and participants engaged. Dramas usually consist of a sequence of scenes through which a story unfolds, human relationships change and problems are explored. If there is no variety in pace or emotional pitch, if there is no tension or suspense, no contrast between one scene and the next, then we are just as likely to get bored as if we find the characters and their preoccupations uninteresting. Similarly, in classroom drama, if the subject matter is inappropriate, if the children are kept seated on the floor for too long, if talk is emphasised at the expense of other activities, or the sequence of tasks is disconnected and unfocused, then interest will quickly wane and the experience will fail to engage the children dramatically. When planning their own drama lessons, teachers would do well to remember that good class teachers and good dramatists work along the same principles. Just as playwrights and directors structure their material in order to vary and deepen the involvement of their audiences, teachers structure their lessons with similar intentions for their classes.

We have discussed these principles because they are important themes that will surface again and again as we explore them in the different examples of our classroom practice. They are by no means exhaustive and many other aspects of drama will be highlighted and discussed as they arise in examples drawn from the classroom. The chapters that follow are meant to provide you and your class with comprehensive introductory activities in drama. The sequences of lessons and exercises should make explicit how the activities described relate to the cultural practice of drama and to the drama curriculum as a whole. The structure and layout of the book are intended to help you develop the confidence and expertise that you and your children need to combine with your tacit understanding of drama in order to fashion its elements into meaningful, educational experiences that match the demands of the primary school curriculum.

In *Chapter 1* we explore the relationship between drama and games and provide a number of examples of games that you might use with different age ranges and for different purposes within a drama lesson. The chapter concludes with a list of strategies to help with the organisation and control of games, all of which can be applied to the management of drama activities in general.

Chapter 2 describes in detail a range of activities that you can use to plan drama lessons using a story as your starting point. As in the previous chapter, we offer guidance to help you focus and manage these activities and vary them to suit the educational needs of different groups and age ranges. Some initial words of advice concerning the planning of a drama lesson are offered by way of a conclusion.

In *Chapter 3* we turn our attention specifically to drama in the early years. We propose a planning structure to encourage you to make full use of the home corner to stimulate dramatic activity. We then take you step by step through an early years drama lesson, giving a full explanation of the principles and strategies which guided the structure of the session and the management of the learning.

Chapter 4 offers several examples of how you can plan for drama as part of your cross-curricular topic work and we suggest a framework for such planning. We end the chapter with a close look at a particular teaching skill, that of questioning, and provide guidance as to when and how you might use certain types of questions in a drama lesson.

Chapter 5 examines the connection between drama and literacy with specific reference to the National Literacy Strategy now established in English Primary Schools.

In *Chapter 6* we concentrate on the place of performance within the primary drama curriculum, offering a rationale for its significance in building and celebrating community and describing in detail two performance projects, one of which was devised with children in Year 6, the other with children in Year 2.

We conclude the book in *Chapter 7* by addressing the thorny issues of progression, continuity and assessment in primary drama. We try to suggest a framework that is both flexible and coherent, one that you will be able to adapt to suit your own particular circumstances. The chapter concludes with advice as to how the assessment, recording and reporting of drama within the primary school can be both manageable for the teacher and rewarding for the children.

Chapter 1

Beginning drama with games

A number of publications have promoted the broad educational advantages that can be derived from games and have shown how different games can, for example, help children develop group sensitivity, encourage social coherence or enhance speaking and listening skills. Many teachers of young children recognise the value such games can play in the personal and social curriculum of their classrooms, incorporating the more reflective of them into circle time activities and the more energetic into drama or PE activities in the hall. While not disputing the educational validity of games, some drama specialists are uneasy when they become too closely identified with the drama curriculum. Games can become a substitute for drama, being easier to organise and readily enjoyed by children; and they can, by implication, place drama too firmly within the area of personal and social education, ignoring its nature as an art form and neglecting the contribution it can make to other areas of the curriculum with 'harder' learning outcomes.

There are, however, certain deep connections between games and drama, as well as some clear distinctions, but because these connections are often presumed rather than explained, teachers sometimes remain only partially aware of them. We will, therefore, begin this chapter with an attempt to clarify what some of these connections are and explain how games can help meet a number of aims and purposes specific to drama teaching. We will then describe a variety of tried and tested examples of such games and offer advice as to how they can be varied and made progressively more challenging. The chapter will conclude with a list of suggested strategies for organisation and control, specifically aimed at students and less experienced teachers.

Games and how they relate to drama

We have argued that, through imaginative play, children are experimenting with and learning how to manage the core elements of drama, those of time, space, people, action, objects and subject matter. As teachers, you are already skilful managers of these elements in your everyday class work and so, by implication, you might be expected to have no problems managing them in drama. The difference is, of course, that, in drama, teachers must first of all *suspend* the normal operation of these elements and manage their transformation from everyday meanings into more playful, *dramatic* meanings. The simplest and most straightforward way to manage such transformations is through games.

Games relate directly to drama in several key ways:

- both types of activity depend upon the human potential for play and suspend the normal operations of time, space, identity, and action;
- space, time, people and actions gain symbolic meaning in games as in drama and our ability to participate in them depends upon our ability to read and understand these meanings;
- both games and drama begin from states of equilibrium which are deliberately disturbed by the creation of a tension or a series of tensions. These tensions are what drive the action and are only finally resolved at the conclusion;
- both are structured around rules and conventions. In games these rules tend to be explicit whereas in drama they normally remain implicit;
- both depend upon forms of emotional and physical engagement as well as cognitive involvement;
- both use a similar range of strategies to sustain interest. These include: the establishment of a clear focus of attention; the fostering of a set of expectations; suspense; the creation and release of tensions; the use of contrast and surprise; and the framing of the activity within a limited period of time.

By way of an example, let us describe and then analyse a common classroom game, playable with children from five years upwards, in order to see how it fits the criteria listed above.

Fruit Salad

1. Chairs are placed in a circle, with one chair in the middle. There must be no spare chairs.
2. Children sit on the chairs and the teacher goes round the circle naming each child in turn APPLE, ORANGE, PEAR; APPLE, ORANGE, PEAR, etc.

3. The child (or teacher) in the central chair begins the game by calling out either APPLE, ORANGE, PEAR or FRUIT SALAD. If she calls out APPLE, all those children given the name APPLE must leave their chair and find a different one. She may also call out APPLES AND PEARS, ORANGES AND PEARS, etc. At the words FRUIT SALAD, *all* children must swap chairs.
4. The aim of the game is for whoever is in the centre to enter the circle and to be replaced by the player who fails to find a chair, whereupon the game starts again.
5. None of the players is allowed either to move into a chair directly next to them or back into the chair they have just vacated.

In this game, children's ordinary identities are suspended as they are given a new name and a clear role which involves, in turn, a clear set of actions. For the duration of the game, children should *only* perform the demands of the role. The rules of the game spell out these demands, specifying when children are supposed to sit and listen and when they need to move and find a different chair. The chair at the centre becomes particularly significant. It symbolises something different from those chairs in the circle, not because of its appearance but because of its isolation, that is to say, its *position in space*. Just *what* it represents is clearly ambiguous. It is the chair that isolates a child from the group, the chair that is to be avoided at all costs; but, if a child ends up in it, she can briefly experience the thrill of being in control, of determining how the game is next to proceed. It is therefore not only a lonely chair but also a powerful chair, analogous in this sense to the throne of a king or the chair behind a head teacher's desk! As soon as the game is concluded, however, the chair and the space around it lose their symbolic meanings and hence their power.

The game is enjoyable only if the players submit to its power and their enjoyment depends upon the suspense generated by the tensions inherent to the game's structure – waiting to hear which fruit is called and then waiting to see who will end up in the central chair. These tensions and their release serve to engage the players emotionally with the game and energise their active, physical participation. Finally, there is always the unexpected that can happen: two players might sit in one chair at the same time, for example, or the same player might end up in the centre on two successive occasions. These elements of surprise add to the enjoyment by altering the game's repetitive structure without disrupting it, but the players will become bored if the game continues for too long. Part of the successful running of a game, therefore, is knowing when to stop it.

In the ensuing chapters we shall explore how these same elements can apply to a drama lesson but, before looking at more examples of games, we think it will be useful to list the other advantages they can offer you when teaching drama.

- Games can provide important signals that drama time is about to happen. They immediately signal a change in the use of space, a change in the energy level and a change in the usual classroom relationships.
- They not only signal such changes but can be used to control them. So a highly active game may help channel children's latent energies if the drama follows immediately upon an extended written activity. On the other hand, a listening game played in a circle might serve to tune children into an atmosphere of quiet concentration after a long and noisy playtime.
- Games can help children explore, define and share the drama space and can encourage them to experiment with their bodies and voices within that space.
- You can select games to introduce certain themes, emotions or relationships which will later be explored in the drama. *Fruit Salad*, therefore, could prelude a drama where power and loneliness are significant themes.
- Very importantly, because they depend so explicitly upon rules, games foreground the importance of such rules. They make possible the discussion of rules and the need for groups to stick to them once they have been agreed. Their role in the social education of children can lay the bedrock for successful drama activity.

The rest of this chapter will provide examples of a variety of games under headings which relate chiefly to their organisational features.

Games which involve movement in space

The following games are suitable for playing in a large space, such as a school hall. We have found that, as well as being good warm-up activities, they perform one or more of a number of functions important to learning in drama:

- they encourage children to explore the limitations and the possibilities of movement inside a given space;
- they help children learn how to share this space with others and how to relate to others in a variety of playful ways;

- they explore how space, and people or objects in space, can have symbolic and therefore dramatic meanings.

When planning to use a game, you should be clear about which of these functions you wish it to fulfil and why they are relevant for that particular lesson. The suggested ages are meant to apply to the average class but, as there is no such thing as an average class, they are offered solely as guidelines. The possible variations for each game are offered as an aid to progression, so that you can not only vary the game but also make it more challenging, in particular for older children.

1. Share the Space (age 6 upwards)

Ask the children to share the drama space equally, without touching the walls. Tell them that, on a given signal, they are to walk through the space, trying to maintain their share of it. Every now and then call 'Freeze!' and comment on how well the children are managing the activity.

☞ *Points to consider*
Initially children will automatically circulate in the same direction and gravitate into the centre of the hall. Encourage them to think consciously about the space, to seek it out actively, to change direction and walk into space wherever it appears. They will soon become adept at this activity but, in the early stages, they can, if necessary, reposition themselves in the space after each freeze.

❖ *Variations*

- Try the same exercise asking children to run, or look over their left shoulder as they walk backwards, or change speed as and when you signal it.
- Ask each child to choose someone in the class whom they will keep an equal distance from, or as far away from as possible, without letting them know. At the end of the game, tell them to touch the child concerned on the shoulder.
- Ask children, in their own time, to stop and hold eye contact with someone before resuming their movement through space. They must do this three times, at which point they are to find a space, sit down and quietly wait until all of the class has completed the activity.
- Tell children they can freeze at will into a shape inspired by a story they have been listening to or by a drama you have recently been working on. As soon as a child does this, count to ten, by which time

the rest of the class must freeze in appropriate ways that will complete the picture. Instruct the class that, if more than one child freezes at once, they can choose which of the pictures they wish to attach themselves to.

2. Tails (age 5 upwards)

Distribute PE bands to all the children except three and tell them to tuck the bands into their shorts or skirts to make a 'tail'. The three children without tails then attempt to catch one. As soon as they do, it becomes their own and the children now without tails become the chasers.

❖ *Variations*

- Let the three children stay as chasers for a minute. At the end of the minute, count how many tails each has caught.
- Hand out four sets of bands, each of a different colour, thus making four teams. Give each team a minute as chasers to see how many tails they can catch.
- Same, only let a team take on the role of 'protectors', attempting to block the chasers from the chased. As blockers, they are not allowed to physically touch anyone.

3. Beans (age 5 upwards)

Ask the children to spread out in space, then call out the names of various types of bean. Each bean must have its own action or gesture, agreed in advance; for example, at the call of 'jumping beans', the children must jump up and down on the spot; at 'runner beans', they run on the spot; at 'string beans', they join hands in a line; at 'baked beans' they huddle together in groups of five or six. Other types of bean might include: broad beans; French beans; coffee beans; jelly beans.

4. Sharks and Islands (age 5 upwards)

Spread hoops or mats on the floor. Tell the children that each is an island surrounded by a sea in which they are to go for a swim. When they hear you call out 'Sharks!' they must 'swim' to one of the islands for safety. Agree with the children in advance how many each island can hold. As the game continues, progressively take away the number of islands to make it more difficult for children to find safety.

☞ *Points to consider*

With very young children, keep the number on each island as low as three. Go around each island and have the class count aloud with you to check that there are only three children on each.

❖ *Variation*

The children who fail to find an island can become sharks and attempt to block swimmers from finding safety. The 'no touch' rule must apply.

5. Huggy (age 6 upwards)

Ask the children to move quietly through the space as in Game 1. As they do so, call out the word 'Huggy', followed by a number – 'Huggy 5' or 'Huggy 4' etc. After each call, the children must quickly get into group hugs of that number. Check the numbers in each group before resuming the game.

6. Follow my Leader (age 7 upwards)

Place a hat on one of the children and tell the rest of the class to line up behind. When the music begins, the child wearing the hat leads the way around and about the room, making a pattern of repeatable movements as he travels. The children in the line must do as he does. After an appropriate length of time, remove the hat and immediately place it on to the head of a different child, calling out 'Change the leader'. Those children in front of the new leader must break off immediately, joining the line behind him, and the game continues.

❖ *Variations*

- Different types of music will generate different kinds of movement.
- Provide a theme, e.g. animals at the zoo, emphasising that it is movement, not noise, that you are looking for.
- Ask the children to form a circle rather than a line so that when you change hats there will be no need for the line to reassemble. This would suit younger children.

7. Knights, Dogs and Trees (age 5 upwards)

Select a child to face the wall and be caller. The rest of the class must now run around in the space until you call 'Freeze!' At this point the children must freeze in the shape of either a knight, a dog or a tree. Now ask the caller to choose and call out one of these categories. Should she call out 'Knights', the knights are to remain frozen while the rest of the class resume running through the space. When you next call 'Freeze!' the knights may remain frozen as knights or may choose to change their shape. As soon as all the children are once more frozen into their chosen shapes, ask the caller to call once again and the game continues.

❖ *Variation*

Negotiate different contrasting shapes for the children to freeze into. These can relate directly to a story or a drama you are working on, for example, 'Hunters, Wolves and Trees' in the case of *Little Red Riding Hood.*

8. Explore the Space with your Body (age 9 upwards)

Repeatedly count from one to ten. For the first count children are to travel through the space in any manner they wish; for the second count they must remain frozen, for the third count they travel again, for the fourth remain frozen and so on. For the duration of the game, the children should attempt to cover as much of the space's three dimensions as possible. While frozen, they should concentrate and try to feel themselves as part of the whole space.

❖ *Variations*

- Use atmospheric music to influence the quality of the movement.
- Provide an imaginary context for the space which relates to the drama lesson – a forest, a desert, an underground kingdom, an alien planet etc.

9. Fill the Space with your Voice (age 9 upwards)

Get the children to move about the space chanting loudly as they do so, attempting to fill every corner of the room with their voices. Lead them in the chant, which should be simple, such as 'Hey, hey, hey ...'

❖ *Variations*

- Vary the chant.
- Ask children to stand still in a space, and conduct the chant, varying the volume by raising or lowering your hand.

Games for pairs and small groups

The following games, as well as fulfilling the aims listed at the start of the previous section, make demands on children's powers of concentration and cooperation, which they will need for improvised pair work and group work in drama.

1. Mirroring (age 7 upwards)

Ask the children to sit facing a partner and to decide which one of them is A and which B. Tell them that A is to begin slowly making a pattern in the air using only one arm. B must try to mirror the pattern exactly. When you call 'Change', the action must continue uninterrupted, with B this time taking the lead.

☞ Point to consider
Make it clear to children that you should not to be able to distinguish the leader from her reflection. The leader, therefore, must not try to trick or lose her partner.

❖ Variations

- Concentrate on other parts of the body – the face, for example, or the legs.
- Children can stand and use any parts of their body.
- Children can travel across the floor as they work, always being aware of where other pairs are working and moving.
- The leader can make a short sequence of movements and stop, whereupon her partner follows her. In this way, the sequence is repeated afterwards, rather than simultaneously. This allows for the movements to have more pace and variety and calls for the use of memory.
- As above, only the leader introduces speech and/or sound with her movements, varying their tone and volume. There need be no logical sequence between one set of movements/words and the next.

2. Show Me (age 9 upwards)

Ask children to choose a partner and to sit in space, facing one another. When you give the signal, A must start telling B about what she did the previous weekend. At any moment, B can say 'Show me!' whereupon A must get up and perform the action she has just narrated before sitting down once again and continuing the story. You can emphasise that this story can be either true or a complete invention. When you call 'Change!' B is to take over the narrative from where A has left it and can develop it in any way she likes.

☞ *Points to consider*

- The actions need to be performed within the limited space each pair is working in.
- Depending upon the class, you may wish to subtly contract out certain kinds of action before the game starts!

3. Sculpt your Partner (age 7 upwards)

A is the clay, B the sculptor. B moulds A into different positions by gently pressing the part of the body she wishes to move and by applying slight pressure to stop it. When you call 'Change!' the children swap roles.

❖ *Variations*

- Sculpt your partner into a particular statue, an image from a story.
- A group sculpts a volunteer into an image taken from a particular moment in a drama. More than one child can be sculpted if the image calls for it. Different possibilities for this image can be encouraged.

4. Group Letters (age 9 upwards)

Put children into groups of seven or eight, whereupon they are to organise themselves into the form of whatever capital letter you call out. They are to remain on their feet, so it is only the sum of their relative positions in space which will form the letter. The letters would thus be 'read' by someone positioned above the space.

❖ *Variations*

- Tell the children they have to do the activity in silence, communicating through eyes and gesture only.
- Organise the groups across the space. If there are five groups, call out a five letter word such as APPLE. Each group must try to work out for itself the letter it should form so that the five groups together spell the word.
- Call out a letter and the whole class must organise itself into it without speaking.

5. Group Shapes (age 9 upwards)

This is similar to the above, only children must use their bodies in groups of three or four to create *vertically* letters or shapes such as 'Star' or 'Eiffel Tower' – lifting, holding hands, positioning their bodies on different levels, etc.

6. What Are You Doing? (age 10 upwards)

Ask the children to sit in circles in groups of about eight and number them in sequence 1 to 8. Number 1 is to begin by entering the circle and miming an everyday action, for example riding a bike. Number 2 must then ask 'what are you doing?' in a genuinely puzzled fashion. Without hesitation, Number 1 must reply by saying something completely different from the action, such as 'Tying my shoe lace' or 'Painting the Mona Lisa'. Number 2 must then immediately take his place in the middle of the circle and mime the action suggested by his answer, whereupon Number 3 asks Number 2 'what are you doing?' and the game continues. Groups can signal when they think the answer given is not sufficiently different from the action by giving a loud group groan.

❖ Variation
Play it with the whole class seated in a circle.

Circle games

Circles are symbolically a very important shape in drama, particularly when the teacher sits among the children. They temporarily transform the various social hierarchies and groupings of everyday classroom reality into one, shared, egalitarian space. The circle can signal that, within it, you will suspend your normal teacher's role as 'Keeper of the Answers'. It can also suggest that everyone in the circle must share responsibility for the success of the activities that take place within it.

1. Rounds (age 7 upwards)

Begin a sentence 'This morning ...' and complete it, for example, with the words '... I had marmalade on my toast'. Each child in the circle must now complete the same sentence in a different way. If any children do not wish to do this, they can say 'Pass', whereupon the sentence moves on to the next child without recrimination.

❖ *Variations*

- The sentence can begin in any number of ways and children can be encouraged to lie outrageously (in other words, to use their imaginations).
- Rounds are useful for recapping on work done in a previous session. You can ask the children to say one thing they remember about the lesson, or about the story of the drama so far.
- Games such as 'I went to market and bought some ...' are a type of round. Children need to recall what everybody else in the circle has bought before adding their own particular purchase to the list. It can be played by passing a basket around the circle.

2. Pass the Squeeze (age 6 upwards)

Sit in the circle with the children and tell them to join hands and close their eyes. Gently squeeze the hand of the child sitting on your left. When the child feels the squeeze, they, in turn, must squeeze the hand of the child on their left and the squeeze is passed around the circle in this way until it is returned to you.

Other passing games

- Chinese Whispers, where children pass a whispered message.
- Pass the Clap, where children can be asked to try and keep the rhythm and volume constant.
- Pass the Mask, where a child mimes putting a mask on her face, gruesome or comic, and then passes it to the child next to her. This child copies the expression, wipes her face clean, puts on her own mask and the game continues.
- Pass the Shoe, where you clap and count rhythmically **1**, 2, 3, 4; **1**, 2, 3, 4, etc., emphasising the beat on the count of one. As you chant 'One!' the child holding the shoe passes it to the child on her left. The rhythm for passing can be varied **1**, 2, 3; **1**, 2, 3, etc.
- Pass the Invisible Ball. This can be thrown across the circle and children can be encouraged to feel its weight as they catch it, to bounce it before passing it on, etc. You can insist that it becomes suddenly very hot, or very cold, or very heavy, or as light as a balloon, etc.

3. Pass the Tambourine (age 5 upwards)

Ask a child to sit in the centre of the circle with his eyes closed while the rest of the class sit in the circle with their hands behind their backs. They then pass a tambourine around the circle, behind their backs, as quietly as possible. When you call 'Stop!' the child in the centre must open his eyes and point to the child he thinks is holding the tambourine at that moment.

☞ Points to consider

Very young children tend to signal with their face and their body language when they are hiding the tambourine. By asking the child in the centre 'How did you know who it was?' you can draw attention to this and encourage the children to disguise their body language – an elementary acting lesson!

4. Sharks (age 7 upwards)

Tell the children to stand in a circle, facing inwards. Begin yourself as the shark by saying a child's name 'Mary' and walking towards her, arms outstretched and eyes focused on her. Before you reach her, Mary must say a different child's name 'Tyrone' and approach him in a similar fashion. Now Mary is the shark and you drop your threatening posture and take Mary's place in the circle. Tyrone, in turn, must say the name of another child and approach her as the shark and the game continues. The aim is not to be eaten (i.e. touched) by the shark.

❖ Variations

- After a short period you can introduce a second shark into the circle, then a third, etc.
- You can insist that a boy must approach a girl and a girl a boy.

5. Songs with Actions (age 5 upwards)

Teach the children a song with actions to accompany the words, such as:

In a cottage in a wood	*(draw cottage and tree in the air)*
A little old man by the window stood.	*(place hand on forehead above the eyes)*
He saw a rabbit hopping by	*(do hopping movements with hand)*
Come knocking on his door.	*(mime knocking)*
'Help me! Help me!' the rabbit said,	*(outstretch arms)*
'The farmer wants to shoot me dead.'	*(mime farmer with pistol)*
'Come little rabbit stay with me	*(beckoning gesture with arm)*
And happy we will be.'	*(mime cuddling rabbit)*

❖ *Variation*

Repeat the song with the first line silent, replaced only by the gestures; then repeat again with the first two lines silent, etc. until the whole song is 'sung' silently.

Games which suggest stories

Unlike drama, games do not tell stories but some of them *suggest* possible stories and hence a possible drama. The following games are good examples of this.

1. The Farmer and the Fox (age 7 upwards)

Ask the children to stand in a circle and choose one of them to be the Fox, who must then leave the circle and face away from it. Choose one child to be the Farmer without letting the Fox know who it is, then make a gap in the circle and place a cuddly toy rabbit at its centre. The Fox now must enter the circle through the gap and as soon as he touches the rabbit, the Farmer can chase him. If the Farmer catches the Fox, he immediately becomes the Fox himself. Whoever manages to make it back through the gap to the Fox's den wins the game.

2. The Magician and the Maze (age 9 upwards)

Divide the children into groups of four or five and line them up alongside one another in straight rows, instructing them to position themselves an arm's length from the children immediately in front of them and to their left. Explain that they are now the walls of a Magician's Maze; that when the Magician calls, the walls will change; that they will represent this by first of all stretching their right arm to touch the shoulder of the child in front of them and at the word 'Change!' dropping their right arm and stretching to touch the shoulder of the child to their left. In this way, the walls can change a number of times. Now choose two children, one to chase the other through the Maze. As the Magician, call 'Change!' at will, or choose another child to perform this role.

3. Keeper of the Keys (age 7 upwards)

Sit the children in a circle and ask for a volunteer to sit blindfolded on a chair in the centre. Now place a large key under the chair. Ask if any child in the circle would silently volunteer to attempt to retrieve the key. If the keeper in the centre at any point hears a noise and points successfully in the direction of the child approaching, she must return to the circle to be replaced by another silent volunteer.

❖ *Variation*

The keeper can hold a rolled up piece of sugar paper. The child is out only if the keeper manages to hit him with it.

This last game is very adaptable for suggesting different stories. You might introduce the keeper as a monster, guarding the door to a secret cave whose treasures the children can only uncover by capturing the keys. When using a drama to suggest a story in this way, it is far better to introduce the game *as a story* rather than by explaining its rules. The drama activities in the next chapter begin with a version of this game which you can introduce in the following manner:

> 'We are the animals of the forest, gathered around a clearing, watching. We have many skills, which human beings do not have; we can see in the dark and can move silently over the forest floor. And tonight we need those skills for one of our friends is being held prisoner by a vicious and cruel Hunter. There he sits, on a tree stump, in the centre of the clearing, with his club in his hand, guarding the keys of the hut in which he has locked our friend. He senses we are near and is waiting for one of us to approach so he can swing the club and kill us. But, unlike us, he is afraid of the dark. He cannot see and dare not move from where he sits. Which of us has enough courage to enter the clearing and try to steal the keys, I wonder? Whoever would like to volunteer, raise your paw in the air.'

The teacher then chooses one of the volunteers and the game begins.

This use of story effectively changes what was a game into a piece of theatre. *Through the story* the space is transformed within the imaginations of the participants into a forest clearing; the chair into a tree stump; the player into a Hunter; the roll of paper into a club; the children into forest animals; the time into the dead of night. The story implies very strongly what the rules of the drama are, and the behaviour of the keeper and those trying to steal the keys are explained and given emotional significance. These dramatic transformations engage the participants much more deeply in the game than if they were absent, with the result that the tension becomes tighter, the suspense greater. Furthermore, the children in the circle are given a possible right of entry into the action; as audience, they are also potential actors. In other words, they are invited not only to witness the action but also to take responsibility for it. But the game (or scene) also leaves a lot of questions unanswered. Who is the prisoner? Why has the Hunter captured her? Why do the animals want to rescue her? What will happen if the animals manage to release their friend? It therefore implies a history and a possible future, both of which can be speculated upon and explored. All the elements of classroom drama are, in fact, here.

Some strategies to help with organisation and control

1. Have any resources you will need to play the game ready and at hand.
2. When playing a game for the first time, have the instructions written down in clear and logical stages as a prompt.
3. Never start an activity until children are properly ready. This normally means that they should be still and silent.
4. When giving instructions to very young children, keep them short and give them one at a time. 'Everyone stand up ... good ... now, fingers on your lips ... right, quietly tip-toe into a space' etc.
5. Have clear and consistent verbal signals for starting and stopping a game and make sure children understand them before you begin.
6. Have a range of strategies for obtaining silence that avoid you raising your voice. These are particularly important when children are working in pairs and groups. A common strategy is to tell children that, whenever they see you with your hand in the air, they must stop what they are doing, put their own hand in the air, and wait quietly for you to tell them what they are to do next.
7. Explain to children that, in drama lessons, they will sometimes choose for themselves who they will work with and that sometimes you will choose for them. Think carefully about when such choices are appropriate. A mirroring game, for example, may best be done with a friend. There are no easy answers to deal with the child with whom no one wishes to work. Over time, however, as children become more and more used to working for short periods of time with lots of different children, the problem can diminish.
8. If you fear that certain children in the class will not work well with their first-choice partner, you can try the strategy 'Choose a partner ... now choose a different partner' before you begin the game.
9. When putting children into groups, the most common method is to sit children in a circle or in a group, number them accordingly and direct each group into the space where they are to work. But be careful! If

there are 28 children in the class and you want them in groups of four, you must number children from one to seven, not from one to four. Numbering children from one to four will, in this case, give you four groups of seven, not seven groups of four!

10. Before beginning work in pairs or in groups, ensure that children understand the limits of their own space and that they appreciate the importance of not intruding into the space of other groups.

11. Present rules and skills as challenges to children and always look for opportunities to use praise. When you do praise children, make it clear what you are praising them for. Insist, for example, that learning to share the space as you move within it is difficult and praise the class when they do it well. If you have high but realistic expectations, children will learn to respect your praise, so don't offer it if it isn't deserved.

12. If some children are spoiling a game for others, don't let the game continue but don't make the whole class suffer. If necessary, sit the class down and discuss the need for a new rule. 'We'll start the game again, only this time let's see if we can play it without anyone bumping into anyone else. Do you think you can all manage that?' Presenting the rule as a challenge rather than as a sanction is important. If certain children persist in flouting this new rule, you can withdraw them from the game with the words 'I think you'd better come and have a look at how the game is supposed to be played'. After a short time, you can negotiate their re-entry into the game, subject to their demonstrating that they now know how to play it properly. If they manage this, quietly praise them later, away from the attention of the whole class.

Chapter 2

Beginning drama with a story:
The Forest Child

Stories are what provide dramas with their substance: the story a drama tells is the key to what the drama is about. Primary teachers do not need reminding of the power and significance of stories in children's learning. Apart from their potential for language enrichment, it is through the particularity of stories that children apprehend and think through ideas and issues of human significance. Stories can thus provide a teacher with ways of accessing important areas of the spiritual, social and moral curriculum; and drama can help children linger among the ideas contained within a story's imagery, to engage more fully with the world the story creates. Similarly to the way that *Cathy Come Home* brought the issue of homelessness into the forefront of British public debate in the mid-1960s, a drama can activate concern among children and can thus be far more effective than classroom discussion in encouraging them to explore the issues a story raises. With primary aged children, the right story can be the most powerful hook into drama.

We believe that using an existing story for drama work presents several advantages for those of you unused to drama teaching:

- a story can provide a clear thematic focus to help you link the drama work into your overall curriculum planning;
- many of these activities can be experienced in short doses within the classroom to allow you and the children time gradually to develop confidence together;
- the drama will not be such a leap into the unknown, for the story will provide you with given characters, places and events around which you can build the work;
- it can help you relate drama work directly to text objectives in the National Literacy Strategy.

Literature for young children is a booming industry these days, and there are so many stories available for primary school teachers to select from that knowing which stories lend themselves to successful drama can be difficult. This chapter will take just one story, *The Forest Child*, by Richard Edwards and Peter Malone. The full written text of the story is included as Appendix 1 and we suggest that you read it now before continuing with the chapter. The story has certain narrative features that lend themselves particularly well to exploration through drama.

- It is superficially a very simple fairy tale with a happy ending, but, like many such tales, it contains certain ambivalent qualities in its character-isation, in the events it relates and in its moral themes. It therefore raises significant questions which are left unresolved – about human relations with nature in general and with animals in particular; about what constitutes useful knowledge; about conformity and non-conformity. Such unresolved questions are the teacher's stepping stones into drama.
- Although utopian in its promise of a happy ending, it is neither trivial nor over-sentimental. It remains engaging and mysterious, with strong atmospheric and visual qualities.
- It has a potential after-life, being open to further interrogation, and is responsive to questions of the 'what if ... ?' nature.

The story is suitable for children throughout the primary years but particularly for those in Years 2, 3 and 4. The age ranges for the particular drama activities are indicated and the aims of the sequence are four-fold:

1. to encourage you and your class to begin to work with and learn to manipulate the elements of dramatic form;
2. to show how drama can help children dwell within a story, getting to know it well, and thus explore its content and its atmosphere;
3. to illustrate how drama can be used for children to explore the issues of human significance that the story suggests;
4. to provide you with the experience of using drama strategies which can be adapted and transferred when planning for drama around other stories with children throughout the primary age range.

Many of the activities below can be done in the space available inside a classroom and are, for the most part, relatively self-contained, to allow you the opportunity to select one or two to try out for yourself as part of your English teaching. Others could be incorporated as part of the music or dance curriculum. They have, however, been sequenced in a logical order and could, for the most part, be organised into drama sessions in a school hall. An introduction to issues related to planning a drama lesson is therefore included at the end of the chapter. As with the previous chapter, variations to each activity are suggested for either younger or older, more experienced children. The activities themselves are structured around a variety of drama strategies or conventions, the names of which are highlighted within the text and descriptions of which can be found in Appendix 2. These conventions can be used to structure drama work for children of all ages and many of them will resurface with further examples in later chapters.

Activities

1. 'Keeper of the Keys' (Year 1 upwards)

Play the version as described on pages 14–15.

2. Previewing the story (Reception upwards)

Gather the children together. Ask the questions that the game raises, listed in the previous chapter, and listen to the answers the children offer. Explain that you are going to read a story which offers an explanation and show the cover of the book, an illustration of the Forest Child with the Wolf, Bear and Beaver. Ask the children what the cover tells them about the Forest Child before you begin to read the story.

☞ *Points to consider*
Movie previews are designed to provoke interest in a film without giving too much of the plot away. Both the questioning related to the game and to the book cover should be seen primarily in this light, as a means of creating suspense, stimulating interest in the story that is to follow and hence maximising the children's powers of concentration.

3. Presenting the story (Reception upwards)

Read the story slowly, showing the pictures as you read. Play some suitably atmospheric music as you read, (such as the track *Wolf* from the album *Bones* by Gabrielle Roth and the Mirrors).

☞ *Points to consider*
- Picture books are often a good resource for drama because, like drama, they use a combination of visual images and words to convey the meaning of the story. The added layering of music over the narrative in effect provides a soundtrack, which can deepen the atmosphere of the tale and brings its telling closer to children's experience of film drama.

- An alternative to reading is storytelling, another way of bringing the experience of a story closer to drama. As a storyteller, a teacher can hold eye contact with her audience and is free to use gesture and facial expression, particularly when relating the speech of the different characters. Even if the story is learned off by heart – and it is often better if it isn't – there is an apparent improvisatory quality in the telling which has something of the immediacy of dramatic speech. The best stories for telling are those which come directly from the oral tradition, such as those found in the collections of fairy tales and folk tales listed at the end of the book. Figure 2.1 is intended to help those teachers who are unused to learning and orally relating stories and is based upon advice given by Bob Barton in his book *Tell Me Another.*

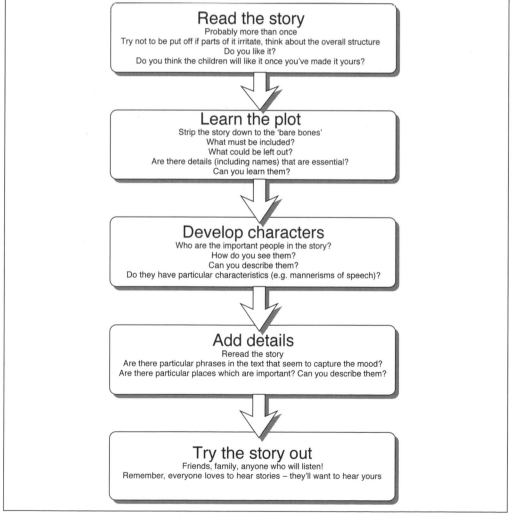

Read the story
Probably more than once
Try not to be put off if parts of it irritate, think about the overall structure
Do you like it?
Do you think the children will like it once you've made it yours?

Learn the plot
Strip the story down to the 'bare bones'
What must be included?
What could be left out?
Are there details (including names) that are essential?
Can you learn them?

Develop characters
Who are the important people in the story?
How do you see them?
Can you describe them?
Do they have particular characteristics (e.g. mannerisms of speech)?

Add details
Reread the story
Are there particular phrases in the text that seem to capture the mood?
Are there particular places which are important? Can you describe them?

Try the story out
Friends, family, anyone who will listen!
Remember, everyone loves to hear stories – they'll want to hear yours

Figure 2.1 Adapted from *Tell Me Another* by Bob Barton

4. Acting out the story (Year 1 upwards)

Form the children into a circle. Introduce them to a 'story stick' (an old walking stick or staff). Explain that you will now retell the story and that, as you do so, the children will act it out in the space within the circle; so, for example, when you say 'Once upon a time there was a Forest Child ...', any child who wishes to take on this part can raise their hand. Whoever the stick points to will then enter the circle and perform the actions of the Forest Child as you relate them and ditto for the other characters in the story. Explain that, when you wave your stick slowly over the stage space, it will clear and fresh volunteers will be chosen to continue the action. Make it clear that, as the holder of the story stick, you are in charge; that you will do your best to ensure that everyone who wants to join in will have the chance but that they may have to be a little patient. These are the rules of the game.

☞ Points to consider

- This activity is an example of how to change the energy level of a lesson, in this case from one of serious and quiet attentiveness to rumbustious activity and laughter. It considerably lightens the atmosphere of the story but such contrasts and changes of rhythm are necessary to sustain interest and later activities will return children to serious reflection.
- The story stick is endowed with a certain magical property, like a wizard's wand or Prospero's staff. As a visual mark of the storyteller's authority, it is an early introduction to the symbolic power of objects in drama and is also used here as a control device to help demarcate real time from drama time.
- The activity makes it clear that, although a story told may be set in the past, when dramatised it happens before our eyes, as if in the present.
- As drama is about action happening now, within space, the teacher will need to re-adapt the text to emphasise physical actions if the children are to know how to respond to the narration. So whereas the story says simply 'One day a Hunter came into the forest ...' the teacher needs to say something in the manner of 'One day, a Hunter walked slowly and quietly into the forest, carrying a gun and looking all about him, peering up into the trees above his head, and into the bushes at his side', etc. These new, surprising details, and the way the actors respond to them, sustain the interest both of those watching and those performing.

- Encourage the children to create physically the scenery of the tale – the trees of the forest, swaying gently in the wind, some short and stubby, some tall and slender; the bushes with their sharp thorns that tug at the Hunter's coat; the big, solid door of his cottage. As well as being a lot of fun, this introduces them to the importance of the body in drama, to how it can represent a myriad of symbolic meanings, and develops their confidence in improvising spontaneously with their bodies.

❖ Variations

- As children gain experience of this way of working, you can have volunteers share the storytelling process with you.
- With children aged 4 and 5, you can narrate and act out sections of the story with the whole class; everyone can be the Forest Child, the Bear, the Wolf, the Hunter, etc. at the same time.
- With children in Year 6, the class can be divided into groups of about six, each with a large sheet of paper and a felt-tipped pen, and be asked to sequence the events of the story in ten numbered sentences. Each group can then sit in a semicircle in front of a clearly defined space and the sheet can be used as an aid for one of the children in the group to act as narrator while others in the group act out the story. Many children of this age, particularly those used to drama, will be able to meet the challenge of entering the stage space spontaneously, without putting up their hand, but the narrators can use story sticks as a control device if the teacher thinks it desirable. These can consist of large rolled up sheets of paper.
- You can add dialogue to the narration with the convention that the children repeat it in the manner in which it is spoken. With more experienced classes, the actors can be required to improvise dialogue. This can be signalled by the narrator saying, for example, 'and the Hunter looked at the Forest Child and said ...', pausing for the Hunter to speak.

5. Making a map of the story (Year 2 upwards)

Put children into groups of about four, each group with a large sheet of white paper and a selection of crayons or large felt-tipped pens. Ask them to make a map of the story, so that anyone looking at it can see where the important incidents happened. When completed, children can be asked to compare them.

☞ *Points to consider*

- Drama and the making of drama is essentially a communal activity and involves participants in negotiating shared understandings of what is significant and how it should be represented. This exercise introduces children to such negotiation of meanings.
- If stories organise events in time, art organises them in space. Drama, of course, organises them in both time *and* space and the activity allows the children to concentrate upon this aspect of spatial organisation.

❖ *Variations*

- Some groups of children may need extra support and will need to be guided by the questioning of a teacher or a classroom assistant.
- Drawing here is being used functionally, inasmuch as the artistic quality of the maps is not at issue. However, it could be the first stage toward the making of a whole-class wall display, where different children take responsibility for illustrating characters, features or events. Children can also write short extracts from the story in their own words, or lines of dialogue, which can then be attached to the display in the appropriate place.

6. Creating the forest through sound (Year 3 upwards)

Look at one of the maps the children have designed and discuss what sounds might be heard in various parts of the forest – those of the stream, those of the wind in the trees, the whistling of the birds and the slithering of snakes in the bushes, the chopping of wood near the Hunter's cottage, etc. Have a variety of musical instruments (pitched and unpitched percussion, recorders) and discuss/try out which instruments best capture the various sounds. Divide the children into groups of about four or five, each with a particular group of sounds to create around a specific location, and provide each group with appropriate instruments. Have them play with and practice the sounds and discuss with each group as they do so what it is they represent. Then tell the children that together you are going to transform the room into the forest and organise with them where each group should place itself and, if possible, darken the room. Take on the part of the Forest Child, narrating as you walk through the forest: 'The Forest Child loved the sounds of the forest. She would often linger by the stream and listen to it as it trickled over the rocks and to the fish as they splashed on its surface ...' Indicate to each group, through gesture and eye contact, when they are to begin and end their contribution.

☞ *Points to consider*

- Here **sound collage** is being used to conjure up the dramatic world, a common technique in live theatre. The children are both audience and performers in this short scene, which will only work if they abide by the rules of conventional theatre, not making any sound other than those related to their performance. They need to understand and agree to do this before the performance, which can then be discussed for its effectiveness and perhaps tried again.
- Darkening the room is a way of creating atmosphere and will be greatly enhanced if some simple stage lighting, with a green-coloured gel, is added to the effect. Transforming the light is another way of transforming the everyday space into a dramatic space.
- The darkened atmosphere and the rules of performance create the tension here. You can add an element of suspense by not telling the children in advance the order in which you will approach the groups.
- Your narration should reach a natural conclusion in order to restore a sense of equilibrium – perhaps the Forest Child finds a spot where there are no sounds and, in the silence, falls asleep.

7. Creating the forest through movement (Year 4 upwards)

Prior to this activity, perhaps as part of your class work, with children discuss and compile a list of those animals which might live in the forest. Of the list you compile, choose five or six whose movements will be interesting to explore and prepare two movement verbs for each: *twist* and *slither* for a snake, perhaps; *swing* and *turn* for a monkey; *swoop* and *glide* for an eagle. Some classes will be able to help their teacher develop this list. Begin the lesson with a game of *Follow my Leader*, using some of these words and movements, then put children into groups and share the animals and the movements out among them. Tell children to choose a partner from within their group with whom to experiment with different ways of performing the movement suggested by the verbs. Then ask them to find a space in the room with their partners and to remain still within it. They are the animals of the forest as dawn breaks and a new day begins. Play the music you used for the reading of the story and narrate them through some action:

'As dawn broke, the first to leave their hiding places were the snakes; twisting and slithering, they moved slowly and silently into the open, over the floor of the forest, through the long grasses and the dead leaves, underneath the bushes and around the tree trunks and quietly, quietly back into their holes. Next to venture out were the eagles ... '

☞ *Points to consider*

- The actor's vocabulary lies within the body as well as within speech and, for many young children, expression through the body comes more readily to them than expression through words.
- The representation of animals need not be twee or babyish. It has a strong tradition within the performance traditions of the First Nation cultures of America and has been seen in critically acclaimed productions such as Peter Brook's *The Conference of Birds* and the various theatrical versions of George Orwell's *Animal Farm*. However, asking children to move like animals will generally lead them into unhelpful clichés, writhing on the floor like a snake or scratching their armpits supposedly like a monkey. Concentrating on aspects of movement will lead them away from an unreflective depiction of the obvious and help them explore new possibilities of improvisation and representation.
- It is difficult for younger children to memorise and repeat movement motifs very accurately. Children from Year 4 onwards can generally be presented with this challenge and given time to work out a motif that they can perform in unison with their partners. Further challenges can be added to help them enhance the movement quality; for example, they can be asked to vary the level (the height) of their motifs; they can be asked to add a quality of lightness or heaviness, depending on the size of the animal, etc.

8. Showing the worst moment for the Forest Child (Year 2 upwards)

Put children into groups of four or five and ask them to discuss what they think is the worst moment in the story for the Forest Child. Ask them to create a **still image** or **tableau** of that picture with their bodies, explaining that each member of the group must be in it and that the picture should show quite clearly what is happening and why this is such a bad moment for the girl. Have each group present their image to the rest of the class in turn, asking the audience in each case what they can read in the image and how they can tell it is such a bad moment.

☞ *Points to consider*

- The still image emphasises how drama communicates through visual signs and is a very good way for children to begin examining in detail how meanings are made in drama by people relating to each other through space. It is an example of how we suspend real time in drama, giving ourselves pause to gaze and reflect and to inquire into human behaviour.
- While the children are working on their images, move around each group, questioning and suggesting if necessary how they might make their meanings clearer, often by altering small details such as eye contact or spatial distance between characters.
- The emotional quality is an important point of focus in such images and reinforces the fact that dramatic performance seeks to engage on the levels of thought *and* feeling.
- Clear rules need to be established for the showing and interrogation of these images, so that those being watched can feel secure under the gaze of their classmates. It is the teacher's job to ensure that each image is shown only when it is ready to be shown and to remember that what matters is the clarity with which each conveys meaning. Guide the questioning and comment so that they focus on issues relating to these meanings.

❖ *Variation*

Still imaging is a very popular and flexible strategy in classroom drama. More examples of its use will be given in later chapters and references to further publications which explore its potential are included at the end of the book.

9. Questioning the Hunter (Year 2 upwards)

Gather the children around an empty chair and ask them what they know about the Hunter. Then ask them why they think he hunts and why he might have acted as he did toward the Forest Child and the boy. Tell them that, in a minute, they will be able to find out from the Hunter himself. Prepare with the class the questions they might ask him and explain that, when you sit in the chair, you will become the Hunter, and will remain as the Hunter until you stand up again. Explain, too, that the Hunter will be the one who speaks first. When you sit down, adopt a fairly hostile body posture and give the children a few seconds to read your body language before telling them that you haven't much time, so could they please get on with the questioning. Respond to their questioning as you see fit with replies that you believe will provoke the children into voicing their own opinions about how the Hunter should or should not have behaved.

☞ *Points to consider*

- This technique (known as **hot-seating**) is the simplest and most controlled way for a teacher to take on and perform a different identity in a drama lesson and for a class to get used to her doing so. There is no need for you to put on a different accent or to change your voice; in this exercise, the *attitude* you display is what matters.
- The introduction to this activity is intended to help children avoid questions, such as 'How old are you?' and 'Have you got a dog?' Although they may be viable in themselves, they are not helpful to the drama as they are not focused around its central concerns.
- It will help if you think in advance what questions you will encourage the children to ask and prepare the kind of answers the Hunter might offer – in other words, rehearse a little before performing. Your answers need to be provocative enough to engage the children emotionally and hence sustain their interest.
- It will aid children's language development if you answer some of their questions with questions of your own – 'Well, what do you suggest I should have done?'
- Avoid being really nasty! If you shout, children will very often laugh as a protective measure.
- End the activity as soon as you think fit, certainly within ten minutes. When you have finished, get out of the chair and ask the children what they thought about the Hunter and why. This clearly demarcates the fictional reality from the everyday reality and younger children, in particular, will readily enter into the game of discussing what the Hunter said as though you genuinely weren't present at the time.
- As children become accustomed to it, they can begin to sit in the hot seat themselves, either for the whole class or in small groups.

❖ *Variations*

- Introduce the activity through a technique sometimes known as **role on the wall** or **role on the floor**. Here, the outline of the Hunter is drawn on to a large sheet of white paper and the teacher acts as scribe while children offer everything they know about the Hunter to be written inside his outlined form. The questions they would like to ask are then written outside the form. After the hot-seating, new facts they have learned about him can be added to the paper, which can be used as a resource to aid written work or further drama work.

- With children in Years 5 and 6, you might play the Hunter more subtly. Through his body language and his speech he can be represented in a very different way from the Hunter of the story, which he might explain as a misrepresentation of what really happened. As a Hunter, you perform an unpleasant but necessary job, and are humane in your methods; you were only trying to help the Forest Child and never shouted at her or hurt her, etc. This is an especially good approach to stories whose stereotypical representations you wish to problematise.

10. A meeting of the animals of the forest (Year 2 upwards)

Gather the children into a circle and ask them which animals they think live in the forest apart from the Bear, Wolf and Beaver. Scribe their answers on to a large sheet of paper, then ask them, 'Who is the wisest animal in the forest?' (the Owl, perhaps, or the Badger). Ask the children to think which of the animals listed on the paper they might pretend to be and to imagine how the other animals of the forest might describe them. If necessary, discuss possibilities for Wolf, Bear and Beaver – Wolf is known as the fast one, or the fierce one, etc. Tell them they may be any forest animal apart from Wolf, Bear or Beaver. Then introduce yourself as Owl 'and I am known as the wisest of animals'. Go around the circle and children in turn introduce themselves in this way. When this is done, inform them that you have called them together to discuss a problem.

> 'This is the first time we have met since our friends Wolf, Bear and Beaver freed the Forest Child and I am troubled. We have taught her to live with us but she is not one of us. We may need to let her go to live among her own kind. She has already brought the boy and the Hunter. I have spoken with her and she wishes to stay with us. We will be sending her back against her will. Bear, Wolf and Beaver wish her to stay, of course, but they are her close friends. I wish to hear the advice of those animals who are not so close to her.'

It is important that the ensuing discussion airs the problems thoroughly. As teacher, don't let the children reach an easy decision. Argue all the reasons she should leave – that humans bring death to the forest, etc. *Do not use this as a forum to reach a decision but as one to air the issues.* Conclude the meeting when you judge that the children have had enough;

thank the animals for sharing their ideas and say you are going away to reflect before making your final decision. Come out of role and ask the children what they think the Owl might decide.

☞ *Points to consider*

- This activity is, in fact, creating a sequel to the original story and is, of course, reminiscent of Disney's version of *The Jungle Book*.
- Unlike the hot-seating exercise, a **formal meeting** (or **meeting in role**) gives the children the chance to take on a role and the discussion is clearly focused around a problem which will allow them to shape future action rather than interrogate past action.
- Although the children are in role as animals, they are exploring a very human problem, namely how far should the individual be required to submit to the interests of the group? If the children all want the Forest Child to stay, which is highly likely, then you must urge them to consider the very real dangers that this might bring to the majority of the forest creatures.
- The ritual of the meeting is a strong control device. As its convener, you can choose who is to speak next; ask individual children what they think and why; insist that they speak one at a time and listen to one another; and close the meeting at any time.

11. Revisiting the sounds of the forest (Year 3 upwards)

Tell the children that, while this meeting has been in progress, the Forest Child has been wandering alone through the forest which has been her home for as long as she can remember. She knows she might soon be asked to leave it forever and, as she visits the places she knows so well, the river where she swims, the bushes where the juiciest berries grow, it is as if she can hear words of advice in the air around her, telling her why she should stay or why she should leave, or reminding her of the things she used to do here. Ask children to form themselves into the groups they were in when they created the sounds of the forest, only this time they are to whisper the words the Forest Child might hear in each place. Give each group time to work out what these might be and to practise them together before organising the performance as described in Activity 6. This time, however, walk through the forest silently, telling each group to whisper their words clearly as you approach them.

❖ *Variation*

- This use of sound collage can be organised in a form known as **conscience alley**, where children are formed into two lines between which a child can be led with her eyes closed to listen to what the different voices are saying.
- A more challenging activity is to have the children repeat their musical phrases and incorporate the whispering they have devised within them.

12. How might this new story end? (Year 4 upwards)

Form children into groups of five and suggest that this new story could have a happy or a sad ending, or an ending which is a little of both. Ask them to decide in their groups what they think this ending might be and to act out their ideas. Go around each group and provide any help needed and, when children have done this, tell them to prepare a **short play** to show what this ending is. Everyone must have at least one line of speech but no-one is to have more than two. Have them rehearse this within a specified time limit then have each playlet presented in succession, insisting that there be no speaking outside of the drama. When this is done, bring the children together to discuss the kinds of endings they have envisaged.

☞ *Points to consider*

- When children act out their ideas in groups, they need not be presented for others to see. If they are, they need a very clear structure and focus. The limited use of lines provides such a structure and helps children select what they consider to be of most significance.
- Presenting the scenes in succession while insisting on silence establishes and contains the special atmosphere of drama time and encourages children to treat each other's and their own material with respect.
- Ask children to watch one another's work carefully and to be prepared to talk about some of the things that they liked and why they liked them. This will not only build up children's self-esteem but can also help develop their powers of criticism within a protective environment.

❖ *Variations*

- This exercise is tightly framed and should avoid the problems which can arrive when children make the plots of their plays too complicated. When this happens, you can ask the children concerned to choose the twenty seconds of action which is the most significant and, if necessary, have them relate to the class the full intricacies of the plot after their presentation.
- Older children can be asked to write down their scripts rather than perform them. The written scripts can then be exchanged so that children have the challenge of interpreting another group's text. The teacher might here introduce the conventions of script writing, including the use of stage directions.

Planning a drama lesson: some basic considerations

Issues related to planning are covered in detail in Chapter 4 but it is worth considering some basic principles at this point. If you were to plan a drama lesson using some of the activities described above, you would need to consider carefully:

- whether the activities matched the children's age and experience;
- whether you had planned control strategies which were clear and clearly understandable to the children;
- whether the sequence of activities you chose sustained a clear and coherent focus;
- whether your intended learning outcomes could be clearly stated;
- whether the sequence of activities provided sufficient rhythm, variety and pace to the lesson.

The first two principles, relating to match and control, have been integral to the work described so far. However, those relating to the focus, the learning outcomes, and the rhythm of the lesson as a whole need some further exploration before we begin, in the next two chapters, to consider examples of drama lessons taught throughout the primary age range and across the curriculum. So let us suppose that you are planning to teach *The Forest Child* as a story-based topic to children in Year 4 and that you intend to use a fifty-minute drama session, timetabled in the school hall, to introduce it. The lesson is to be structured around the first five activities described above: the game *Keeper of the Keys*; the previewing and reading of the story; acting out the story; mapping the story. The children themselves are relatively unused to this kind of work.

Now the *focus* of a drama lesson is often the exploration of an issue or a key question of human significance. For example, the meeting of the animals of the forest explores, through the particular situation of the Forest Child, the more general question of how far communities can tolerate those who are significantly different. Such key questions are further discussed in Chapter 4, where the issue of planning is returned to in rather more detail. In this instance, however, the lesson does not focus upon a key question; it will lay the groundwork for such work by introducing children to the story, engaging their interest in it and ensuring that they get to know it thoroughly. At the same time, as the children are unused to drama, you will be aware that such activities as the enactment of the story will introduce them to the possibilities of physical representation. There is therefore a twin focus, on issues of content (related to the story) and issues of skills and form (related to the medium of drama). Issues of skills and form relate directly to what children are asked to make and perform within a drama lesson and just what might be included in this aspect of the drama curriculum is examined more thoroughly in Chapter 7.

This twin focus will be representative of most drama lessons and, most importantly, it should be clearly evident in the *intended learning outcomes* which you list. The clear statement of such outcomes should be an integral part of your planning, phrased in such a way as to ensure that their attainment will be visible. In this way, you will be able to judge at the end of the lesson to what extent children have learned what you wanted them to. With this in mind, we might envisage the intended learning outcomes for this particular lesson as follows:

By the end of the lesson, children will

- be able to name the characters in the story and explain their function in its plot;
- know the order of the events in the story;
- understand the geographical space in which the story happens;
- have explored how they can use their bodies to help tell a story in drama.

The very act of listing such objectives will help sharpen up your pedagogy. For example, it is now clear that, while children are engaged in the mapping exercise, you should tour the groups, helping those who are struggling with their understanding of the environment of the story, noting those who show an understanding and those who may need remedial help. You also need to consider how, at the conclusion of the lesson, you can quickly assess whether your first two objectives have been achieved or not. You could do this by gathering the children in a circle and asking questions such as: 'Who tries to help the Forest Child in this story? How? Who tries to hurt her? How?' Then, opening the book at random, you could ask children to explain which characters they can see in the illustration; what is happening at this moment in the story; who thinks they know what happened on the previous page and what will happen on the next page? and so on. Such activities will help you note those children who would benefit from additional exposure to the story before they continue with further work on it.

The outcome of the final objective is necessarily more difficult to pin down, its intention being to introduce children into a way of working. However, it will still be visible whether children are confident or reluctant and relatively skilled or unskilled in their performance of the task. With all the intended objectives, the assessment of the learning outcomes will enable you to make systematic observations upon which you can match your future planning to the children's capabilities and potential.

In order to address the final principle, the *rhythm and variety of pace* within the lesson, you will need to consider the kind of engagement demanded by each activity – whether it *settles* the children, demanding passivity, concentration, quiet and stillness; or whether it *stirs* them, demanding action, energy, talk and movement. It is helpful to consider a line along which we can position different activities within the lesson according to whether they settle or stir the children, for the rhythm of a successful lesson will be characterised by activities which shift in both directions along this line, creating a rhythm of varied demands – physical, intellectual and verbal.

1. *Keeper of the Keys* has moments of both 'settling' and 'stirring' but demands silence and stillness from most children for most of the time.
2. Previewing/reading the story demands silence, stillness and concentration.
3. Acting out the story demands bouts of energy and activity and condones noise and laughter.
4. Mapping the story demands talk and small motor activity (drawing) while condoning a limited amount of movement.
5. Conclusion demands concentration and willingness to answer questions.

If we consider the proposed sequence of activities in this way, it is evident that an imbalance in the rhythm of the lesson occurs in the earlier activities, where children are required to sit on the floor and concentrate for too long a period. You might decide to begin the lesson with a more lively warm-up before playing the game *Keeper of the Keys* but, in addition, you could consider how to provide some variety between Activity 1 and Activity 2. So, at the end of the game, you might ask the children to consider which animal of the forest they had imagined themselves to be. You could then narrate the return to their dens, which the children would perform through controlled and quiet movement. The place of this den could be specified as the area in front of the teacher's chair. Once the children were settled in this space, they would be ready to hear the story. In this way you would have improved the rhythm of the lesson as a whole, while building upon the imaginative context for the story established during the opening game.

Chapter 3

Beginning drama in the early years

A girl of seven and her four-year-old brother have just been through the gruesome business of house-hunting with their parents. In the tedious trail from one property to another, all of which seem perfectly adequate to the children, they become bored, irritable and confused. When they return home though, they are overheard playing together in the living room of their existing home. 'This is the living room,' says the girl. 'Over here you can see we have got a radiator and down there is an electric plug.' 'I see', replies the boy, 'I like this house.'

This kind of play will be familiar to all teachers and parents of children in the early years. The children have taken the bemusing experience of being shown round one house after another and recast it in a form that they can manage and explore for themselves. To play 'house-hunting', they pretend that their own house (the space) is unfamiliar and different, that they are other people and that the action takes place at an unspecified time other than the present. They maintain these pretences for the duration of the 'game', but frequently interrupt and suspend the game to remind or negotiate with each other about where it should go next: 'Ask me how many bedrooms the house has got' or 'Let's pretend the garden has got horses in it'. The principles of drama which we explored in the introduction echo right through this kind of play: many (although by no means all) children start school with a good understanding of how time, space and people can be managed to create and enact a fiction which is meaningful and enjoyable.

Pretending the garden has horses in it is an important departure. Playing estate agents will quickly become just as dull as the real business of looking for a new house, but the discovery of horses offers new and exciting possibilities for the story that the children are making. The horses may need looking after, they may have escaped from a cruel owner, they may be able to talk, they may have magic powers – suddenly the story of this game looks like it could get interesting.

The value of this kind of play – variously referred to as 'pretend', 'imaginative' or 'fantasy' play – is recognised by many early years teachers.

In many classrooms there is some kind of area set aside for such play. It may be set up as a 'home corner' or it may be set up as some other place, often connected with the theme or topic on which the class are working. If the theme is 'food' for instance, the area may well be set up as a café: if it is 'clothes', a laundry; and if it is 'ourselves', a health centre or hospital. It is interesting to note, given the connections we make between drama in the classroom and its wider cultural manifestations, how significant such spaces are in soap operas and other TV drama: cafés, launderettes, pubs all serve as locations where members of the community can meet, talk and play out their own dramas.

As an early years teacher, you may well have tried to exploit the potential of play in this way but run into two related problems. The first is that the initial excitement of setting up the shop or café seems to wane quickly; the space becomes little used and you can be disappointed by the quality of the play which takes place there. The second problem may arise from the stories that the children create for themselves. An area set up as a café may for instance, at the instigation of a group of children who are playing in it, suffer a break-in. The ensuing game of 'catch the robbers' will no doubt be very exciting for those involved, but will almost certainly disrupt the rest of the class and have precious little to do with the topic of 'food' which the area was supposed to support. This is not to suggest that the stories that children make for themselves are not important and valuable, but we recognise that teachers are required to account for and manage children's learning with clear objectives and outcomes. Planning ahead can develop such clarity and help to ensure that children's play is both structured and purposeful.

Planning for imaginative play

The second of the principles of drama that we outlined in the introduction was that it uses stories to explore issues of human significance. This same principle is also often evident in children's imaginative play, but they will decide for themselves the course of the story and the issues and themes within it that may offer them the most excitement. The challenge for you as the teacher is to plan the layout and resourcing of the area in such a way that it will generate and encourage stories and action which most closely relate to the learning you have identified for your class.

Figure 3.1 suggests some headings under which the area might be planned.

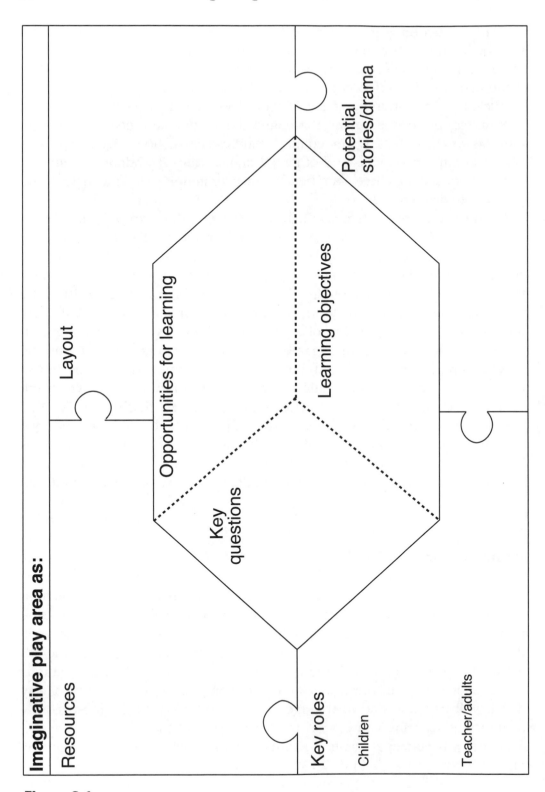

Figure 3.1

Learning objectives/opportunities

Teachers need to be clear about the learning objectives and expected outcomes that they have for children. Working with a nationally prescribed curriculum, you may be given very specific skills, knowledge and understanding which you are expected to develop over a specified period. Incorporating imaginative play as part of the children's experience can be an important way in which you can give the learning a living, human context for the children, making it exciting and relevant. But you will need to be quite clear about your purposes and you will need some means of showing that your intentions are being met. Clear statements about the expectations for children's learning under this section will help to keep the overall purpose of the play area focused and guide decisions about its use and development. The learning which has been identified may immediately suggest a suitable idea for setting up the play area, but where this is difficult it is often helpful to identify the *human* contexts within which the skills, knowledge and understanding are needed. The curriculum may, for instance, demand that children are introduced to a variety of geographical areas and features. Who in the real, human world needs to know about all that? A pilot? An explorer? A travel agent perhaps? Each context would suggest an idea for how the play area might be set up.

Resourcing and layout

Once a decision has been reached about what the imaginative play area will be, the more detailed planning can begin. It is at this stage that you can plan with the class – what suggestions do they have for how the area should be laid out and what should be in it? Not only will this help them feel a sense of ownership and investment from the start, it will also help to make certain that the area feels as real as possible for them and concurs with their own experiences. Children setting up a hospital waiting-room, for instance, suggested that it needed a drinks machine and some magazines to read – they included the objects which best represent their own experiences of such places.

Key roles

When the children go to play in the area who will they be? Who are the people we might expect to find in this place and what sorts of things will they do there? Unless children and teacher are quite clear about this from the start there is a danger of the area losing its purpose and appeal. As well as identifying who the children might be, it is important to think about the roles of teachers or other adults. If adults go and take an active part in the play, who will they be and how will their presence and intervention change and develop the children's ideas? In an area set up as a health centre, an adult may take the role of a patient who is very nervous and frightened about seeing the doctor. Such an intervention demands that children think more deeply about their behaviour as doctors, nurses or other staff and set about the business of reassuring the 'nervous patient'. By taking an *active* part in the play, the adult also gives it a higher status – the area becomes more than just a place where some children are allowed to play when they have finished their 'proper work'; it is an exciting place to be because exciting things happen there.

Potential stories/drama

Once the area is set up, the play can begin. Initially the children will need opportunities for 'free play' in the area, trying out different roles and behaviours as appropriate. But if, as we stressed in the introduction, dramas should not be boring, the same must also be true of the imaginative play area. When everyone has written a prescription, sorted the clothes ready for washing or served the umpteenth cup of tea, what will happen next? How will the children's interest and enthusiasm be maintained and developed, their understandings deepened? Somehow we need to introduce problems, tension and surprise.

In a classroom where the imaginative play area has been set up as a café, the teacher has taken the role of an older member of the community who uses the café as somewhere to meet and talk with her friends. The class have already had the opportunity to meet the role (**hot-seating**) and, through their play, they have seen her go into the café to order food and drink and to chat with the people there. One morning, the teacher tells the class that the people in the café are worried because they have not seen their friend for a few days. The stakes in the play are raised: the children are now faced with a problem in their story and through their actions within their play they can arrive at a satisfactory conclusion.

Opening up the action

Figure 3.2 illustrates how one teacher planned her imaginary play area as a café. An enduring problem of the imaginative play area is that what happens in it is often interesting, exciting and sometimes noisy. If it is one activity among many in a busy classroom, it can be in danger of dominating and

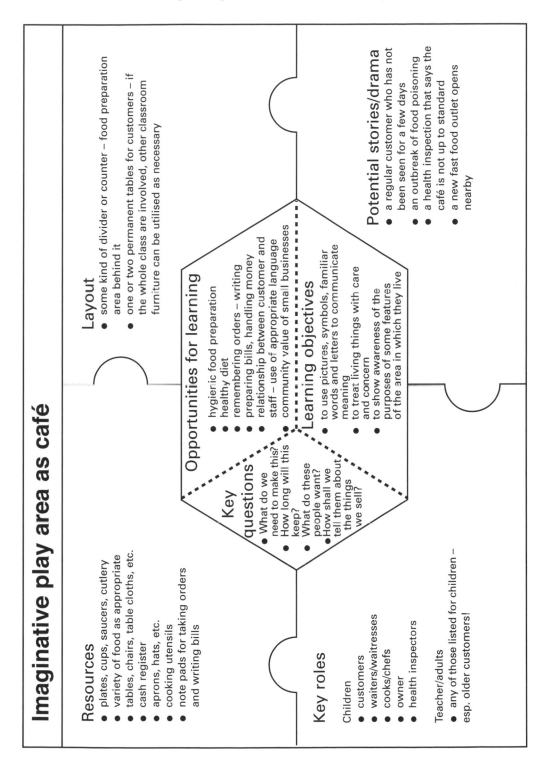

Imaginative play area as café

Resources

- plates, cups, saucers, cutlery
- variety of food as appropriate
- tables, chairs, table cloths, etc.
- cash register
- aprons, hats, etc.
- cooking utensils
- note pads for taking orders and writing bills

Layout

- some kind of divider or counter – food preparation area behind it
- one or two permanent tables for customers – if the whole class are involved, other classroom furniture can be utilised as necessary

Opportunities for learning

- hygienic food preparation
- healthy diet
- remembering orders – writing
- preparing bills, handling money
- relationship between customer and staff – use of appropriate language
- community value of small businesses

Key questions

- What do we need to make this?
- How long will this keep?
- What do these people want?
- How shall we tell them about the things we sell?

Learning objectives

- to use pictures, symbols, familiar words and letters to communicate meaning
- to treat living things with care and concern
- to show awareness of the purposes of some features of the area in which they live

Potential stories/drama

- a regular customer who has not been seen for a few days
- an outbreak of food poisoning
- a health inspection that says the café is not up to standard
- a new fast food outlet opens nearby

Key roles

Children

- customers
- waiters/waitresses
- cooks/chefs
- owner
- health inspectors

Teacher/adults

- any of those listed for children – esp. older customers!

Figure 3.2

distracting children from their other work. One possible solution, particularly when you wish to introduce some new problem or tension, is to open up the area and allow everyone to watch what goes on there. In the example of the old person who visits the café, the class have just finished meeting (hot-seating) the role and they are then invited to see what happens when she goes into the café. Two or three children are invited to take the roles of the people who cook and serve the food and drink and two or three more the roles of other customers. The rest of the class are then invited to watch as the **teacher in role** as the old person goes in, sits, is served and talks with staff and customers.

The parallels between this approach and conventional theatre are obvious. The play area, by opening it up, has become the 'set' on which the action takes place, 'actors' are watched by the 'audience' of other children who form the 'fourth wall' of the space. The advantage of this approach is that everyone can see and hear what is happening and has the opportunity to comment on it afterwards: children can begin to develop their capacity to analyse and comment on dramatic activity.

In the example of the café it is also possible to open the area out so that the whole classroom becomes part of it. In this way everyone can become involved in the story as it unfolds. The most appropriate time to do this would be when the staff and customers learn that the old person has not been in for a few days. They can then work as a whole group to talk and plan what they want to do. Where the unfolding story goes now depends on their collective decisions and their collective actions. To take the children's work on from here we need to have ways of negotiating the next stage, of structuring and organising the action, and of drawing the work to a satisfactory conclusion. In one example, the children agreed that they should go round and call on the old woman to see if she was all right. The teacher retook the role as the children called at her door: she was ill and unable to get out. They organised a visit from the doctor and, of course, plenty of food and drink. The story was concluded when the woman recovered and went back to the café to thank everyone for their concern and help.

In this example, the drama grew out of the children's play in the café they had created. The normal routine of the café and its customers was disrupted when one of them did not appear for a few days and the 'problem' was resolved by the children in their roles as the staff and customers. The story was firmly rooted in the children's own play, but teacher intervention challenged them to follow a particular path. The teacher also worked with the children to give form and structure to the work: planning how the space could be organised; taking an active role when appropriate; and helping to focus discussion about the story and its consequences. As the story grew, it became shared and communal. Such work while clearly rooted in and recognisable as children's imaginative play, also has many of the characteristics of drama which we outlined in the introduction. For both teachers and children it can be a very good place to start.

The figures which follow provide further examples of how teachers have planned for the different uses of the imaginary play area, as a laundry, a health centre and as a forest. In Figures 3.4 and 3.5, gaps have been left in the key areas of learning to enable you to project your own ideas as to what they might consist of.

The drama lesson in the early years

Imaginative play and its associated stories which we have considered so far in this chapter often form part of a pattern of activities in early years classrooms. There may be points where the whole class become involved in the same story, but there will also be a large number of smaller stories of the children's own making, many of which take place without any adult involvement at all. When we think of the 'drama lesson' we tend to think of a 'bigger story' in which the whole class can take an active part. We have already shown in Chapter 2 how published stories can offer a good starting point for drama, and *The Forest Child* would certainly be suitable for children of six or seven. The next example, though, shows how a piece of work can be devised from scratch.

Deciding content

This drama was planned for a class of five- and six-year-old children. They were already working on the topic of 'Toys', but most of the work they had done so far had been based on the technology of toys, their mechanisms and how they work. We were keen to move into the area of 'special' or 'favourite' toys – those toys which so many children have, without which they don't sleep. We wanted to explore what it is that makes some toys special in this way. The class also had a problem, familiar to many teachers and children, of a small number of children who were isolated and found it difficult to relate to others. If possible, the drama was also to address this.

☞ *Points to consider*

- When thinking about the content for the drama, it is important to think about the child's perception of the topic. 'Toys' is often chosen as a topic

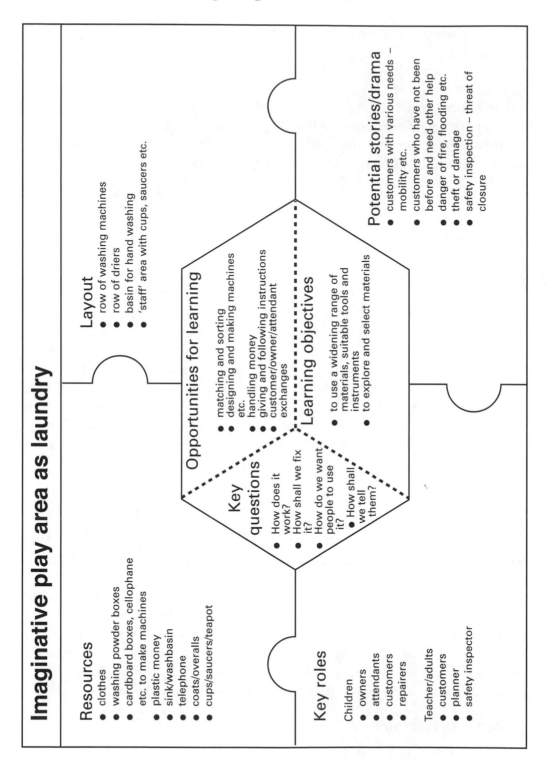

Imaginative play area as laundry

Resources
- clothes
- washing powder boxes
- cardboard boxes, cellophane etc. to make machines
- plastic money
- sink/washbasin
- telephone
- coats/overalls
- cups/saucers/teapot

Layout
- row of washing machines
- row of driers
- basin for hand washing
- 'staff' area with cups, saucers etc.

Opportunities for learning
- matching and sorting
- designing and making machines etc.
- handling money
- giving and following instructions
- customer/owner/attendant exchanges

Key questions
- How does it work?
- How shall we fix it?
- How do we want people to use it?
- How shall we tell them?

Learning objectives
- to use a widening range of materials, suitable tools and instruments
- to explore and select materials

Key roles
Children
- owners
- attendants
- customers
- repairers

Teacher/adults
- customers
- planner
- safety inspector

Potential stories/drama
- customers with various needs – mobility etc.
- customers who have not been before and need other help
- danger of fire, flooding etc.
- theft or damage
- safety inspection – threat of closure

Figure 3.3

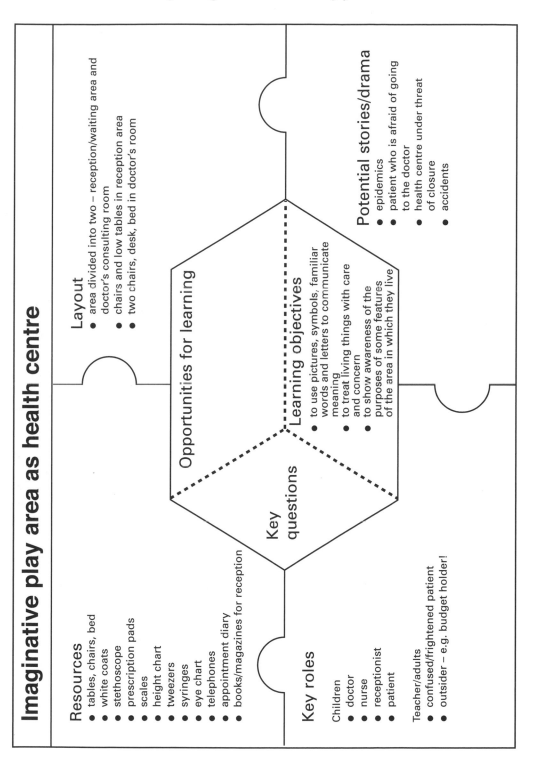

Figure 3.4

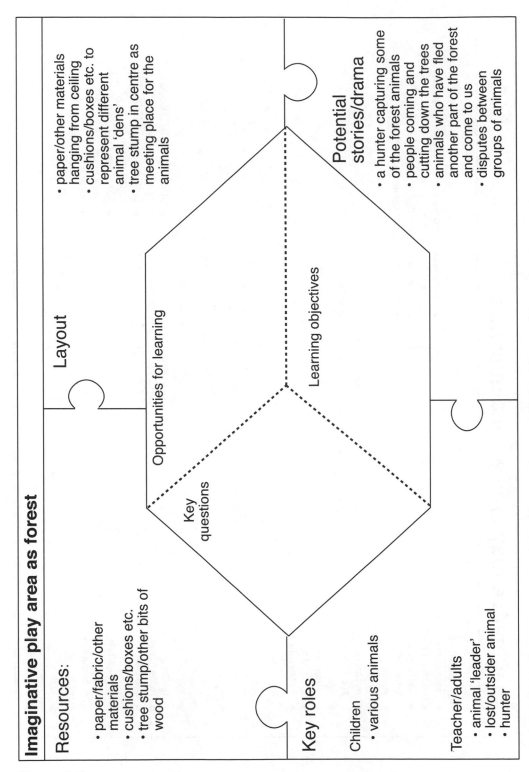

Figure 3.5

because of the opportunities it offers for developing technology work, but this drama focuses on the way in which many children will project human characters and characteristics on to their toys.

- It is important, too, to think about how much experience the children may have had of the content you have chosen for their drama. In this case, it was necessary for the children to have had existing experience of the content even though the drama extended that experience further.

The starting point

The drama begins with the children seated in a circle: they have just finished playing one or two games of the type discussed in Chapter 1. Just in front of her place in the circle, the teacher spreads out a quilt and a pillow which, by the way they are patterned, indicate that they belong to a child. She also places a large teddy bear in the bed. The children are asked to look at the image and talk about what it shows. The simple use of props such as these tells some important things about the story that may be about to take place in this space – children are encouraged to look at and 'read' the image in just the way that we might when looking at a set in the theatre. The children are also invited to suggest names for the child and the teddy. The teacher then tells the children that she is going to be the child in the bed and that they will have the opportunity to talk to her and find out more about the story.

The teacher takes the role of the child, sits up in the bed and answers the children's questions. Through her responses she indicates that she talks to the teddy, that he is a very good friend and that she can tell him anything. She also indicates that she has a suspicion that the teddy has a life of his own when she is asleep: he's never in the same place when she wakes up as he was when she went to sleep. The children may learn a good deal more about the child and her teddy, but these are the key points for the teacher to put across.

☞ *Points to consider*

- When choosing a name for the child, the first suggestions are taken – we don't want to spend the whole lesson debating the issue!
- As with the example of questioning the Hunter in Chapter 2, it is well worth spending time talking about the kinds of questions that will be asked before they begin, otherwise the teacher can find herself sitting in an uncomfortable silence. Preparing some questions with the children beforehand helps the ensuing activity to establish and maintain

momentum but does not preclude children from asking further, spontaneous questions once the activity is underway.

- It is important to establish and maintain the convention that when the teacher sits in the bed she is the child, but when she gets out she goes back to being the teacher – this way, she knows that she can stop the questioning at any point, discuss what has been said and recap on the developing story.

Roles for the children

The context for the story has now been established, but the children need to become *actively* involved in it as soon as possible. The teacher has already hinted that the teddy has a life of his own when the child is asleep. Working from the idea that all the toys in her bedroom come alive when she is asleep gives the possibility of roles for all the children as the other toys. The teacher asks for suggestions about what the other toys might be. As a child makes a suggestion, they are asked to choose three or four other children to be those toys with them.

☞ Points to consider

- It is important to make sure that the toys they represent can be animate – if a child suggests that there are cars in the bedroom, ask if they can be the *drivers* rather than the actual cars, so allowing them to take a full part in the drama. In any work, you need to check that roles children choose for themselves do not exclude them from taking a full part in the subsequent drama.
- As each group of toys is put together, the teacher gives them a 'box' to be in, represented by a PE mat. This is an important device because it organises the space and ensures that each child knows where their 'box' or base is – the toys can be asked to return to their boxes so that the developing drama can be paused, discussed and refocused.
- The children have made their own choices about what kind of toy they want to be within the clear constraints that the teacher has set. Already they can feel that they are having some ownership of the drama and some influence over the way in which it is developing.

Acting the roles

The children now need some time to establish themselves in their chosen roles as toys. They also need to get up and move about. The teacher could use a simple signal for the toys to come alive: 'When I count to three ...' or 'When I clap my hands ...' but the activity is kept within the logic of the story if the children play it as a kind of game. The teacher sits in the bed, when she lies down and 'goes to sleep' the toys can come alive, move around and talk to each other but if she 'wakes up' they must go back to their boxes as quickly and as quietly as they can. An activity like this, with all its echoes of games such as *Grandmother's Footsteps*, is great fun and very enjoyable in itself, but it also allows the children to start engaging with roles as toys and building their own belief in the story.

A role for the teacher

The teacher has already played the role of the child and the children have established themselves as the toys in her bedroom. But their two stories will remain separate because the toys can only become active when the child is asleep. The key to the drama's continuance is for the teacher to swap the roles of the child and the teddy. She tells the children that from now on the teddy will represent the child asleep in bed and the teacher will take the role of the teddy. This will allow teacher and child to become part of the same story and to develop it together. They are now all toys who by some mysterious magic are able to come alive at night. The children are removed from the mundane and everyday into a world which is normally closed to them: the tension begins to mount.

Moving the story on

The children now need a different signal for the toys to come alive. The hall where they are working has the curtains drawn – this is often worth doing with any drama at this stage since it helps to keep attention on the space in which we are working and limit distractions from outside. To signal that it is night and the toys can come alive the teacher simply turns the lights (or some of them) off. This simple use of lighting can change the atmosphere considerably, adding to the sense of mystery and tension, just as lighting changes might in the theatre.

With the space darkened, the teacher takes the role of the teddy and calls the other toys over to her: she desperately needs to talk to them. She speaks in a whisper because she is afraid of waking the child. The atmosphere is very different from the game-playing of a few minutes earlier. She reminds the toys that the child speaks to her most evenings before she goes to sleep. She is very worried because the child seems very unhappy – she has said that she does not like going to school, that she has no friends, and that some children are unkind to her. The teddy is very surprised by this 'because she is always so kind to all of us'. The other toys are asked what they think. They too, of course, can only speak in whispers and must speak one at a time so that they can all hear.

☞ *Points to consider*

- The need for the toys to whisper adds further to the sense of tension. The use of a whisper also indicates that the teddy may be about to confide in them – simple changes in tone of voice like this are often much more effective (and much easier) than putting on an accent.
- Speaking one at a time and not shouting are rules that teachers often try and encourage children to adhere to, but the difference here is that the need for quiet has come from *within* the story: if you feel that it is getting noisy and out of control you can, in your role as the teddy, urge quiet in case the child wakes up.

Working with the children's ideas

As the toys talk about what Teddy has told them, they begin to make suggestions about what might be at the heart of the problem. To do this they are drawing upon their own experiences of school, friends and friendship, but they are doing so at an important distance from their everyday lives. It is, after all, only a story that we have made up together. Although it's only a story it feels very real, and quickly the children want to start suggesting possible solutions to the problem.

As the toys talk, one suggests that they should all go with the child to school so that they can find out what's happening. All the toys could climb into the child's school bag and go with her. It is teacher as Teddy who points out the impracticality of this – the child is bound to notice the extra weight – we could send just one of us who could find out and report back tomorrow night. Inevitably, lots of the toys volunteer, but the teacher as Teddy chooses a child to whom she wishes to give a special status within the drama, not 'the best', but one whom she feels will benefit from taking a higher status role.

☞ *Points to consider*

- Some of the suggestions children make may result in very particular challenges for the teacher: a toy soldier might speak up saying that he and his friends have guns and will go and shoot the children who are not kind. The key to dealing with such suggestions is to work from within the story: it is as the Teddy, not as the teacher, that you need to question the wisdom and morality of such a course of action. It is also important to remember that the toy soldier, not the child, made the suggestion in the first place.

- Many teachers, particularly when they begin working with drama, are concerned that they will not be able to 'think on their feet' fast enough to deal with the children's ideas and suggestions as they come at them thick and fast. In fact, they are often pleasantly surprised by how well they do react and respond, but it is always worth knowing what your 'get out' will be. In this case the Teddy only needs to tell the other toys that the child is waking up and they must return to their boxes: the lights can go on and the drama be suspended for a few moments, if necessary until the next lesson, to give you time to gather your thoughts.

The importance of narration

Once the suggestion of going to school has been made and accepted, the action needs to move away from the child's bedroom. The children (except one), in their roles as toys, cannot be part of the action even though it is a key part of the story so the teacher *tells* what happens:

'Before *** (the child) woke up, the little toy crept downstairs, made her way to the school bag and carefully climbed in. She hid right at the bottom so that she would not be noticed. It was a bumpy ride to school and when she got there the bag was hung in the cloakroom. She waited until everything had gone quiet, then carefully climbed out of the bag. Nobody saw her, but she saw everything that happened at school that day. At the end of the day, she climbed back into the bag and rode home. When the lights went out that evening the other toys could hardly wait to hear what she had to say.'

The lights are turned out, the toys come alive and they wait for the news. Teddy is now only one of the toys, and a heavy responsibility has passed to the child who was the chosen toy. She reports that it is all true, but says she thinks it is all down to one child who is particularly unkind and 'needs teaching a lesson'. She might, of course, have said all sorts of things that could have taken the story in an entirely different direction, but if the story has gained enough momentum and her own belief in it has grown, she is almost certain to remain within its conventions. The story might take a different twist, but it will still make sense and have a logic of its own. Through their discussions, the toys decide that they will all go to school – a few each day so that the child does not notice – hide, and wait for a suitable opportunity to frighten the 'bully' and so 'teach the lesson'. It is the children's suggestion, made within the conventions of the drama, and the teacher has to find some way of seeing it through. The children also need to be in on the action.

Concluding the drama

Rather than really hiding, the children are asked to take up 'hiding shapes' which show how the toys look while they are waiting for the bully to appear. The teacher (as Teddy) says that she can see the bully coming: 'When I count to three we'll all jump out and scare him!' On the count of three all the toys jump up and shout at the bully. No-one has been asked to be the bully – he only exists 'off stage' – but the noise is pretty frightening all the same. The teacher then restores order and asks the toys to go back to their boxes. Again she uses narration:

> 'The toys waited quietly in their boxes until (the child) came up to bed. Then they listened as she spoke to Teddy.'

The teacher retakes the role of the child, sits up in bed and tells the teddy about what happened at school:

> 'You know that boy I told you about, the one who hasn't been kind to me, well, I was out on the playground today and he came running outside crying his eyes out. I asked what the matter was and he said that there had been a really loud noise in the cloakroom and it had frightened him. I told him that when I got frightened by things I talked to you about it and do you know what, he said he's got a teddy he talks to as well! We talked and played together all playtime – he's coming to tea next week and he's bringing his teddy to meet you.'

The children, listening as the toys in their boxes, hear how their action resolved the problem of the story – and the logic of that story has been maintained throughout.

The story could, of course, have taken a number of different turns and been resolved in many other ways. By taking a key role in the story herself, the teacher was able to work from within it, exploring possibilities with the children, suggesting consequences and offering her own suggestions for what the toys might do. For all that, the story was still largely the children's: they helped construct it through their discussion, their decisions and their actions.

The work outlined in this chapter demonstrates how the underlying principles of drama discussed in the introduction can apply with young children. All the work is rooted in children's capacity to suspend the normal rules of time, space and identity, and to play in the imagined worlds that they create. As their play developed into drama, teacher and children worked together to create, structure and enact a story and all were able to contribute to its development.

Chapter 4

Drama in the curriculum

Dramas use stories to explore issues of human significance and, like all stories, dramas have to be *about* something. Because we can suspend the normal rules of time, place and identity, we can make dramas about other people in other places and at other times. Drama gives these stories a form and shape which can make them engaging, thought-provoking and exciting for the children who are part of them: dramas should not be boring.

The demands of a nationally prescribed curriculum put considerable pressure on teachers to 'fit everything in': each subject has its own expectations and makes its own particular demands. Finding the time for drama, however highly you and your class may value it in its own right, can be difficult – the more so if we are going to give the drama time to develop, deepen the children's involvement and understandings, and reach a satisfactory conclusion. But the rest of the curriculum may also be full of opportunities to learn about the lives of other people, at other times, and in other places. Taking some of that curriculum content to use for our drama offers opportunities not only for developing good, exciting drama, but also for children to take a different approach to such content and to engage with it more fully. Such dramas are not only valid and valuable in themselves, they can also be shown to enhance children's understanding of other areas of the curriculum and make their experience of it less fragmented.

By taking content from it, drama can relate to the rest of the curriculum in a number of valuable ways. It is always important to remember, however, that drama explores issues of *human* significance: making dramas about 'electricity' or 'materials' is very difficult, but making dramas about the ways people use such things, particularly if such use leads to human dilemmas and tensions, has much more potential. The examples that follow show some of the ways in which drama might draw its content from the rest of the primary curriculum and demonstrate ways in which children's experience of that curriculum can thus become enriched.

Example 1: The Three Pigs' Homes (Year 2)

This class of six- and seven-year-olds has already done a considerable amount of science-based work about materials and their properties. With young children, the story of the *Three Little Pigs* is often used in connection with this area of work because it deals so directly with appropriate and inappropriate uses of materials.

The class is seated in a circle and the teacher invites two children to perform the moment from the story where the first little pig is sold (or given) the material to build his house. In many tellings of the story, the pig is told that straw will make a good house, yet the children know very well that it will not. The class then talk about the absurdity of building a house from straw alone, and discuss other inappropriate materials. They play a game where each person in the circle completes the sentence, 'The strangest thing you could make a house out of would be ...'. As the game develops the ideas become more and more bizarre and the children enjoy its creative playfulness. The teacher then invites some children to form groups to work on their suggested house. The groups work together to make a drawing of the house, then create a short piece of mime to show the builders at work. They are asked to think carefully about what it would be like to work with their chosen material – would it be heavy, strong, rigid, wobbly, etc.? In thinking, and acting this through, they are referring back to all the work they have done on materials and their properties.

The next stage is to ask each group to think about all the advantages they can for the house they have built. Why would anyone want to live there? How could they 'sell' their idea? The groups are then arranged to make the 'Pigs' Ideal Home Exhibition'. The teacher takes the role of the little pig, comes into the space and visits each house in turn. Each group shows her around and tries to sell her their particular house. From her role as the pig, the teacher can ask questions (often seemingly stupid) which she could never ask as the teacher. She pushes some children very hard with her questioning and gets some valuable insights into their understanding of the work they have done on materials. The story, with its absurd possibilities and bizarre conversations, is also very funny and enjoyable for everyone involved. Finally, the children come out of role and question the little pig about what she saw. She projects that she is very confused – they all seemed so nice and every house seemed to have so much going for it, it's very hard to choose.

☞ *Points to consider*

- Work such as this gives children an opportunity to refocus their understanding of the work they have been doing and place it in a new context. The drama provided children with a way of thinking differently and creatively about materials and their properties, and the teacher gained important insights into their understandings which she could not otherwise have had.
- Although this work was undertaken with quite young children, it is worth noting that it makes greater demands of them than the examples given in the last chapter. They are expected to take more responsibility for its development, working in groups to make decisions about their own houses. There is still a considerable degree of spontaneity, however, and much depends on the quality of the improvised role-play between teacher and children.

Example 2: The People of the Winds (Year 3)

This class of seven- and eight-year-olds has been studying the weather. They have talked about the wind and the good and bad effects it has on the lives of people. In the first stage of the drama they work in groups to think about the good things that the wind does for us. Each group is asked to make a short moving image of the 'good wind' at work: turning the sails of the windmill; pushing the boat along; flying the kite; drying the washing. They are then asked to produce some words in the same sort of form as the nursery rhyme *The House that Jack Built*. A group that has shown a windmill come up with 'We are the wind that turns the sails that turn the gears that turn the stones that grind the flour that makes the bread that feeds the people and keeps the people happy'. The class then form a circle to create the 'Great Gathering of the People of the Winds': a meeting at which the people of the winds celebrate the good that they have done for people and plan the next year's work. Each group comes into the circle and performs their work. At the end of the performances the teacher narrates that, 'One year, the people of the winds are gathering when this happens'. She then runs round the circle and into the centre with the words: 'I am the wind that whips the waves, tears up trees and rips off roofs. I am Hurricane! Can I join the gathering?'

The people of the winds are divided. In trying to decide whether Hurricane can join them they debate what the power of the wind does, what it might mean to be 'too strong', and the wind's relationship with the living world.

☞ *Points to consider*

- The purpose and value of this work does not lie in teaching children the meteorological detail about what goes on in the earth's atmosphere; by casting the winds in this form, children are enabled to reflect and think differently about the power of the wind and of nature in general. This story has a mythological dimension which engages children in a way which scientific fact alone cannot always do.
- The children create the images and words to depict the uses of the wind in stages. At each stage they are given a clear structure within which they can develop their own ideas. Clear constraints can often make it easier and less threatening for children to work creatively.

Example 3: The Saxons and the Viking Raids (Year 4)

In this example, the children start their work by thinking about life in Saxon England: who were the people and how did they live? The children have already done some research in their classroom and, through his questioning, the teacher encourages them to speculate about the everyday lives in a settlement of the time. He then asks them to work in groups to represent these everyday lives in still images: the images are of hunting, fishing, farming, preparing food. The children are asked to show their work and the teacher reviews it with the class, emphasising the points where they show the closeness of the life to the land – this is a good place to live and the people have all they need. The children are then asked to develop their images into a short piece of movement and to think of some accompanying words to express their importance to the people concerned. A group who have made an image of people sowing, for instance, use the words, 'the land is good so the crops grow well'. These images and the words which now accompany them are used to form the basis of a festival or **ritual** in which the people celebrate the harvest and all the good things the land has given them. They are presented to the 'village circle' one at a time, accompanied by music which the children compose and perform. The children also talk about what the other elements of the ritual might be (they have all celebrated the harvest in their own school) and include song, dance and special food. This preparation for the festival is carefully crafted; children rehearse their work and attempt to make improvements so that those watching will appreciate and understand it better.

The teacher then introduces the class to the role of the traveller. He takes this role himself and signifies it by wearing a cloak and carrying a staff or walking stick. He tells the children that he is going to walk among them and

that as he gets close to them they may ask him questions: he will pause by
them and answer. The kinds of questions they might ask are discussed, and
then the teacher begins his walk. He does not look at the children, but
answers their questions as if he is 'thinking aloud'. He is a traveller; he is 'of
nowhere'; he trades with the villages as he moves between them; he is
known and trusted in all of them. Through his answers he projects an image
of someone who is rather distant and mysterious. The teacher then removes
the cloak and talks with the children about how they themselves view the
traveller and how the villagers might view him.

The children are asked to enact their ritual. As the ritual concludes, the
teacher puts on the traveller's cloak and takes up the staff. He then narrates:

> 'At the end of this year's festival the traveller arrives. He is known to the
> people of the village and they always look forward to trading with him
> and hearing the news that he brings.'

The traveller walks to the middle of the circle and begins to speak. He tells
the villagers that he has just come from a settlement further down the river
that has been ruthlessly attacked by raiders. They have burned and laid
everything to waste and he feels certain that they will come here next. The
people must decide what they are to do, but he advises that to try and fight
these people would be useless – he has seen them and they are the most
fearsome fighters imaginable. The traveller leaves the circle so that the
people can decide what action they will take.

The discussion that follows is lively and at times heated. Through the
performance of the ritual, the children have built up enough belief and
investment in the place and the good things it provides to understand how
the people would care about the possibility of its destruction. Some favour
staying and fighting, others wish to flee before the raiders arrive – there
seems little chance of reaching a consensus. The teacher asks the class to
divide into those who want to fight and those who want to flee. They then
work in pairs or threes to create moments of saying farewell – some of these
have a few words in them, many have none at all. The teacher then asks the
'fighters' to make images of how they think they will be when they take on
the raiders: the images, not surprisingly, are of heroism and bravery. Those
who chose to flee are asked to make their versions of how they think the
fighters will be: this time the hall is littered with corpses.

☞ *Points to consider*

- It is important to stress that drama has not been used to teach children
  information about the Saxons. The work might reinforce children's

understanding about what would make a good place to settle and remind them that the Viking raids took place, but its main effect has been to deepen their understanding of the impact that such events might have had on the people who lived at the time.

- The drama explores the ways in which people behave when their community is threatened – deciding when to stand and fight and when to retreat is just as much an issue today as it was then. By taking part in work such as this, children get the opportunity to explore such issues at a 'safe distance' from their everyday experiences, yet can become much more involved than they would through a class or group discussion.
- Although the later parts of the drama are improvised, the ritual is very carefully crafted. At each stage of its development, children are expected to give careful attention to the detail of their work. When crafted in this way, a performance can hold considerable tension as children become committed to 'getting it right'.

Example 4: Building the Reservoir (Year 5)

This class has been looking at the impact of human activity on the environment. The teacher chose the building of a reservoir because it is one of the most attractive 'green' developments and offers some genuine dilemmas about its effect on the environment and the rights and wrongs of building it.

Initially the children are asked to assume roles as 'experts', either in reservoir design and construction, or in marketing such designs to the general public. They are spoken to in role by the teacher, who represents the water company planning their reservoir: the company needs them to prepare a case to put to the residents of the villages which will be affected. Over a period of time, the children work on maps, posters, brochures and models to convince the residents that the reservoir would be beneficial to their interests. They carefully prepare a display in the school hall and are asked to set the hall out as it might be for a public meeting convened to discuss the plan.

The children then look at maps of the area and think and talk about the people who live there. They work in groups to create short scenes of village life – farms, shops, pub – and are then shown a letter from the water company inviting them to the meeting. Each group is asked to create a short piece to show how the residents react to the letter. Still in role as residents, they walk to the village hall and are sent into the meeting a few at a time, look at and react to the display. The meeting is conducted by the teacher in role as the water company's representative. It is heated and unpleasant and the residents plainly don't believe the company's assurances. Discussing the meeting out of role, the children are in little doubt that the plan will go ahead anyway.

The drama then moves to look specifically at one farmhouse that will be flooded when the reservoir is built. The children's work is centred on the farmer who lives there alone. As he leaves the farm for the last time and the sound of the bulldozers is heard, they create moving images of the memories that the farm holds for him.

☞ *Points to consider*

- In this instance, the drama is an integral part of a larger project in which the children are engaged. By working with drama they begin to experience how geographical skills, knowledge and understanding do not just exist in isolation but can have a real impact on people's lives.
- The roles which the children are expected to adopt in the first stage of the drama assume considerable expertise, but the expectation is clearly linked to the work they have been doing and they are well supported and resourced as they prepare their display. Offering children high-status 'expert' roles like this can be a valuable way of raising self-esteem, but it is important to make sure that they have the necessary knowledge and support to sustain the roles so that they are credible for themselves and for others in the drama.
- As the work develops, the children are expected to take on more than one role; and the roles which they play at different times in the drama may well present opposing views. Although this makes high demands of them, it can be a powerful way of encouraging children to consider both sides of an argument. It may be very tempting for the teacher to divide the class in two and ask one half to argue for and the other against a particular case. Debates set up in this way can often become very heated, but there is a danger that children will simply become more deeply entrenched in existing views without any genuine reflection.

Example 5: The Siege of Troy (Year 6)

This class of ten- and eleven-year-olds has been studying Ancient Greece as part of the history curriculum. They are already familiar with the main points of the story of the siege of Troy. They begin by playing a circle game in which each member of the class says 'one good thing about' the person sitting next to them. This leads into some discussion about the qualities which we value in each other: friendship, loyalty, humour and hard work are all mentioned. The discussion then moves on to the kinds of qualities which the Trojans might have valued in each other: the class is introduced to the idea of 'virtues'. In groups, they then make 'statues' (**still images**) to represent the virtues and devise a spoken 'inscription' to go with their work. The teacher then walks among the statues and is reminded of the way in which a good Trojan should live.

As the class enacts the episodes in the story where the Trojans discover and bring in the wooden horse, the teacher is able to refer back to their statues and remind them that they are to show courage, bravery, determination, etc. The teacher also takes on the role of Sinon, the Greek warrior left behind as a 'captive' to convince the Trojans to take the horse into their city. The children create whole-class still images of the Trojans pushing the wooden horse into the city and a further image of the city after the celebrations of victory. They are then asked to return to their original images of bravery, heroism, etc., and each group is asked to make two further tableaux of the ensuing battle between the Greeks and the Trojans. They are then asked to devise movements which link these images together – the teacher stresses the need for precision and control so that the final effect is very spectacular, but quite safe. The linked images are then put together with music and, as the music is faded, the class move to present a final image of devastation and destruction to depict the end of the battle.

The teacher then narrates how the guardian goddess of Troy, Pallas Athene, returns to the city to survey the devastation. As she does so, the bodies of the dead rise up and form new statues proclaiming the new 'virtues' of Troy after the defeat. The class are given time to work and come up with images depicting mistrust of others, fear of outsiders and wariness of deception. There follows a discussion in which the class compare the virtues before and after the defeat and reflect on which are most like our own today.

☞ *Points to consider*

- This work is demanding in terms of the role behaviours expected of the children. They have to take quite abstract concepts like bravery or loyalty and interpret them in speech and action.
- The movement work which is used to depict the battle requires commitment and discipline. It is important for both teacher and class to recognise that creating the apparent chaos of battle needs very careful structure and organisation. This discipline is not only essential for the

safety of everyone involved: the final effect is much more dramatic if everyone is confident and familiar with the structure which holds it together.

- There are complex cultural ideas at the heart of this work. The content of the drama, as well as its form, makes high demands of the class.

A framework for planning to teach drama

Like any other lesson, this kind of drama needs careful planning if it is to be successful. Schools do, of course, have their own conventions for setting out lesson plans but the examples included as Figures 4.1 to 4.5 use a framework intended to encapsulate a thought process through which teachers can work from their broad curriculum planning towards the specific demands of a drama lesson. The format can be completed in note form so that the teacher can keep it at hand while she works with her class. It can be used to plan either a single lesson or a longer unit of work to be taught over two or three sessions.

Learning area

This heading links the content of the drama to a learning area within the curriculum. Often it is the 'topic' or theme in which the class are engaged for the term, half-term or few weeks ahead. There may be a *general* heading like 'weather' or 'homes', but it is also necessary to be more specific about the *particular* area of learning which will inform the drama. In Figure 4.4, for example, the coming of the reservoir was a specific area in which a theme relating to the broader topic of 'The environment' could be explored.

Key questions

Many teachers will already be familiar with using key questions to inform their planning. They encourage research-based approaches to children's learning in which they investigate or address questions rather than simply seek to answer them. Above all, they serve to keep the work focused, reminding the teacher what the work is really about. In planning for this kind of drama it is often helpful to try and identify two or three key questions. One may deal specifically with the chosen content and one may be a bigger question about how people live and behave. In the example of the Saxon drama the first key question, 'What makes a good place to settle?', is very much about the historical content of the drama. The other questions, 'How

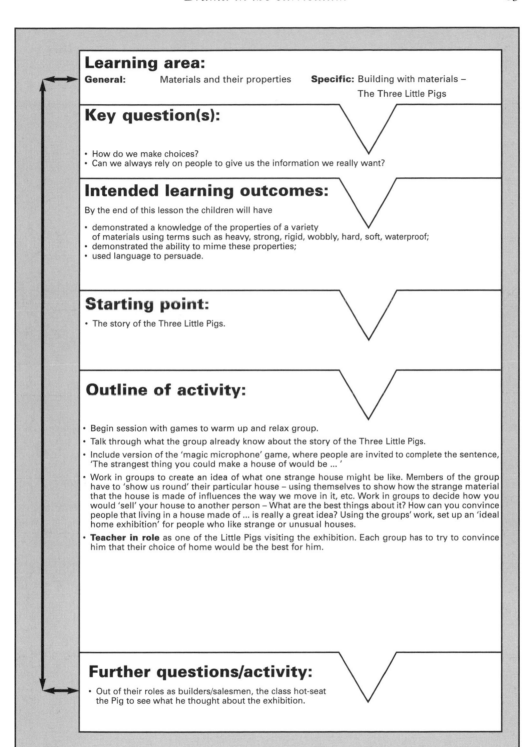

Learning area:

General: Materials and their properties   **Specific:** Building with materials –
The Three Little Pigs

Key question(s):

- How do we make choices?
- Can we always rely on people to give us the information we really want?

Intended learning outcomes:

By the end of this lesson the children will have

- demonstrated a knowledge of the properties of a variety
  of materials using terms such as heavy, strong, rigid, wobbly, hard, soft, waterproof;
- demonstrated the ability to mime these properties;
- used language to persuade.

Starting point:

- The story of the Three Little Pigs.

Outline of activity:

- Begin session with games to warm up and relax group.
- Talk through what the group already know about the story of the Three Little Pigs.
- Include version of the 'magic microphone' game, where people are invited to complete the sentence,
  'The strangest thing you could make a house of would be … '
- Work in groups to create an idea of what one strange house might be like. Members of the group
  have to 'show us round' their particular house – using themselves to show how the strange material
  that the house is made of influences the way we move in it, etc. Work in groups to decide how you
  would 'sell' your house to another person – What are the best things about it? How can you convince
  people that living in a house made of … is really a great idea? Using the groups' work, set up an 'ideal
  home exhibition' for people who like strange or unusual houses.
- **Teacher in role** as one of the Little Pigs visiting the exhibition. Each group has to try to convince
  him that their choice of home would be the best for him.

Further questions/activity:

- Out of their roles as builders/salesmen, the class hot-seat
  the Pig to see what he thought about the exhibition.

Figure 4.1

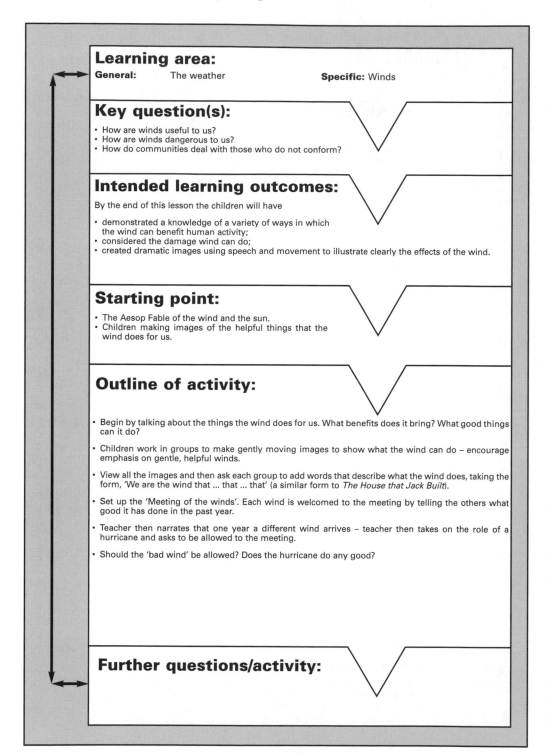

Learning area:

General: The weather   **Specific:** Winds

Key question(s):

- How are winds useful to us?
- How are winds dangerous to us?
- How do communities deal with those who do not conform?

Intended learning outcomes:

By the end of this lesson the children will have

- demonstrated a knowledge of a variety of ways in which the wind can benefit human activity;
- considered the damage wind can do;
- created dramatic images using speech and movement to illustrate clearly the effects of the wind.

Starting point:

- The Aesop Fable of the wind and the sun.
- Children making images of the helpful things that the wind does for us.

Outline of activity:

- Begin by talking about the things the wind does for us. What benefits does it bring? What good things can it do?
- Children work in groups to make gently moving images to show what the wind can do – encourage emphasis on gentle, helpful winds.
- View all the images and then ask each group to add words that describe what the wind does, taking the form, 'We are the wind that ... that ... that' (a similar form to *The House that Jack Built*).
- Set up the 'Meeting of the winds'. Each wind is welcomed to the meeting by telling the others what good it has done in the past year.
- Teacher then narrates that one year a different wind arrives – teacher then takes on the role of a hurricane and asks to be allowed to the meeting.
- Should the 'bad wind' be allowed? Does the hurricane do any good?

Further questions/activity:

Figure 4.2

Learning area:

General: Anglo-Saxons in Britain   **Specific:** Saxon settlement

Key question(s):

- What makes a good place to settle?
- How do communities mark and celebrate the things that they value?
- How do communities behave when under threat?

Intended learning outcomes:

By the end of this lesson the children will have

- demonstrated a knowledge of how the Saxon way of life was different from their own;
- devised and taken part in the performance of a ritualistic piece of theatre to celebrate this way of life;
- sustained a role in order to explore how a Saxon community might have responded to the threat of a Viking raid;
- presented clear dramatic images to depict the effects of such a raid.

Starting point:

- Making a Saxon festival of harvest/thanksgiving.

Outline of activity:

- Begin by discussing what the children already know about Saxon settlements – What would the people need? What would be important to them?

- Work in groups to make still images of daily life in the settlement – review the images and emphasise the way in which the people are dependent on the land around them.

- Discuss the 'elements' that might be included in a ceremony/ritual to celebrate the harvest – work in groups to develop each of these ideas – music? dance? words? movement? special food?

- Bring the elements of the ritual together.

- Introduce the role (teacher) of a traveller who moves between settlements, buying and selling wares. Meet the role by having him walk among the children who may speak to him as themselves (i.e. not as Saxons).

- Work in groups to make images of families or groups getting the news of the traveller's arrival – How do people seem to react to him? Is his arrival welcome?

- Enact the ritual. At the end, the traveller arrives with the news that neighbouring settlements have been raided by Vikings – he is sure that they will come to this settlement next.

Further questions/activity:

- What should the people of the settlement do? Flee? Fight? Try to collaborate?

Figure 4.3

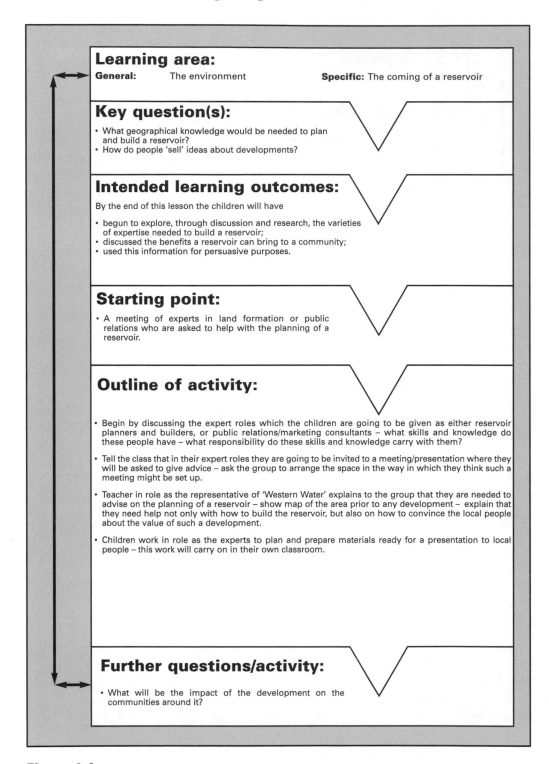

Learning area:

General: The environment   **Specific:** The coming of a reservoir

Key question(s):

- What geographical knowledge would be needed to plan and build a reservoir?
- How do people 'sell' ideas about developments?

Intended learning outcomes:

By the end of this lesson the children will have

- begun to explore, through discussion and research, the varieties of expertise needed to build a reservoir;
- discussed the benefits a reservoir can bring to a community;
- used this information for persuasive purposes.

Starting point:

- A meeting of experts in land formation or public relations who are asked to help with the planning of a reservoir.

Outline of activity:

- Begin by discussing the expert roles which the children are going to be given as either reservoir planners and builders, or public relations/marketing consultants – what skills and knowledge do these people have – what responsibility do these skills and knowledge carry with them?

- Tell the class that in their expert roles they are going to be invited to a meeting/presentation where they will be asked to give advice – ask the group to arrange the space in the way in which they think such a meeting might be set up.

- Teacher in role as the representative of 'Western Water' explains to the group that they are needed to advise on the planning of a reservoir – show map of the area prior to any development – explain that they need help not only with how to build the reservoir, but also on how to convince the local people about the value of such a development.

- Children work in role as the experts to plan and prepare materials ready for a presentation to local people – this work will carry on in their own classroom.

Further questions/activity:

- What will be the impact of the development on the communities around it?

Figure 4.4

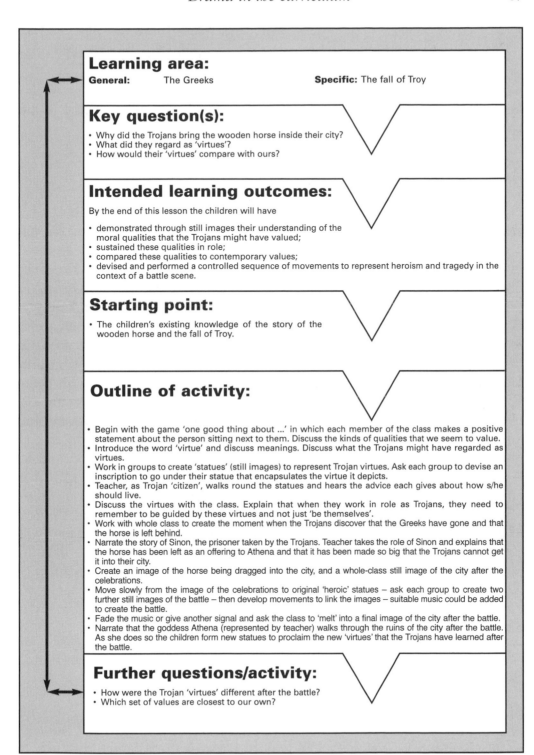

Learning area:

General: The Greeks   **Specific:** The fall of Troy

Key question(s):

- Why did the Trojans bring the wooden horse inside their city?
- What did they regard as 'virtues'?
- How would their 'virtues' compare with ours?

Intended learning outcomes:

By the end of this lesson the children will have

- demonstrated through still images their understanding of the moral qualities that the Trojans might have valued;
- sustained these qualities in role;
- compared these qualities to contemporary values;
- devised and performed a controlled sequence of movements to represent heroism and tragedy in the context of a battle scene.

Starting point:

- The children's existing knowledge of the story of the wooden horse and the fall of Troy.

Outline of activity:

- Begin with the game 'one good thing about ...' in which each member of the class makes a positive statement about the person sitting next to them. Discuss the kinds of qualities that we seem to value.
- Introduce the word 'virtue' and discuss meanings. Discuss what the Trojans might have regarded as virtues.
- Work in groups to create 'statues' (still images) to represent Trojan virtues. Ask each group to devise an inscription to go under their statue that encapsulates the virtue it depicts.
- Teacher, as Trojan 'citizen', walks round the statues and hears the advice each gives about how s/he should live.
- Discuss the virtues with the class. Explain that when they work in role as Trojans, they need to remember to be guided by these virtues and not just 'be themselves'.
- Work with whole class to create the moment when the Trojans discover that the Greeks have gone and that the horse is left behind.
- Narrate the story of Sinon, the prisoner taken by the Trojans. Teacher takes the role of Sinon and explains that the horse has been left as an offering to Athena and that it has been made so big that the Trojans cannot get it into their city.
- Create an image of the horse being dragged into the city, and a whole-class still image of the city after the celebrations.
- Move slowly from the image of the celebrations to original 'heroic' statues – ask each group to create two further still images of the battle – then develop movements to link the images – suitable music could be added to create the battle.
- Fade the music or give another signal and ask the class to 'melt' into a final image of the city after the battle.
- Narrate that the goddess Athena (represented by teacher) walks through the ruins of the city after the battle. As she does so the children form new statues to proclaim the new 'virtues' that the Trojans have learned after the battle.

Further questions/activity:

- How were the Trojan 'virtues' different after the battle?
- Which set of values are closest to our own?

Figure 4.5

do communities mark and celebrate the things that they value?' and 'How do communities behave when under threat?' are much bigger and have wider implications about the ways in which humans behave, then and now. It is well worth spending time thinking about and identifying these key questions because they contribute so much to the future purpose and direction of the work.

Intended learning outcomes

The exploration of a key question may well provide the overall thrust of a drama but teachers need to decide upon clear intended learning outcomes in order to assess what learning has taken place. As we have already discussed in Chapter 2, some of these outcomes should relate directly to areas of content outside the drama curriculum with others relating to those areas of skills and knowledge specific to drama. So, for example, in Figure 4.4, the learning is chiefly located within the area of content; children are meant to learn about the varieties of expertise needed for the building of a reservoir and of the benefits a reservoir can bring. Subsequent lessons, however, as described in Example 4 (p. 59), would include learning objectives specific to children's ability to make and perform drama. In being required to imagine, invent and then play out a public meeting in which local residents debate the catastrophic effects the reservoir will bring to their particular community, the children will need to invent and develop roles applicable to a specific situation and to sustain them for a given length of time in order to explore a problem with a particular social dimension. In Chapter 7 we will see that these outcomes relate directly to suggested end of Key Stage Statements suitable for children in the upper junior years. As with content, the nature of these outcomes will depend upon children's age and experience. Ideally, a school will have in place a framework for progression in drama to enable teachers to set suitably challenging tasks so that their learning outcomes can ensure progressive development in drama. This issue of progression is therefore a key one and it will be dealt with more fully in Chapter 7.

Starting point

In the examples given, each class has already begun to work on the content of the drama within their classwork. But the teacher needs to think through what it is that will engage the children and suggest to them that the story is worth knowing. Stories (as we explored more fully in Chapter 2), poems, pictures, objects can all make good starting points. The teacher may also choose to set up some kind of image (as in the Teddy drama in Chapter 3) to introduce the drama and encourage children to speculate on its possibilities. Whatever starting point we choose, the drama will need to spark interest and get moving quickly.

Outline of activity

In this section of the planning sheet the teacher lists the structures and strategies that she will use to keep the drama moving with sufficient variety and pace. It is important for her to begin the work with a clear idea of what is going to happen and in what order. As she becomes more experienced, she may sometimes move away from the planned activities, particularly as she begins to respond to and work with the children's ideas, but she will feel far more confident with a clearly planned spine of activity, even if she does not always strictly adhere to it. As was emphasised in Chapter 2, the key to planning this section of the work successfully is to think about the overall pace and rhythm of the drama. Will the story keep moving along with sufficient energy to sustain the children's interest? Will the structures used be appropriate and manageable given the age and experience of the children? Will they deepen involvement as the story gathers pace? A selection of the conventions a teacher might use to plan such a spine of activities is provided as Appendix 2.

Further questions/activity

As the work develops, it will generate questions and further issues of its own. It is important to relate the developing activity back to the original purpose of the drama: returning to the key questions will help to keep it focused and limit the possibility of the story getting into areas which, however interesting, have little to do with the teacher's original planning. In the example of the three pigs drama, for instance, the focus remained on materials and their uses as the story moved on to explore how the pig could best be protected from the dangers of the wolf.

Managing the pace and direction of the drama

In all the examples given, the teacher works with the children to structure the drama and give it form. At times the story will be 'live': it will happen in real time and everyone will behave as the people within it. At other times the development of the story is suspended while we discuss it or work on tasks that will take it on to the next stage. Figure 4.6 shows some of the

From within the drama	**Outside the drama**
Teacher in role	**Setting tasks**
➤ **High-status**	• giving instructions
• being 'in charge'	• clarifying instructions
• giving orders	• making the task clear
• running meetings	• giving appropriate guidelines and constraints
➤ **Equal-status**	• allocating time
• joining in discussions and arguments	• indicating ways of listening and seeing for the audience
• making suggestions and observations	• applying a range of conventions to deepen the work
• giving warnings	
➤ **Low-status**	**Reviewing tasks**
• asking for help	
• asking for advice	• 'reading' each other's work
• asking for mercy	• giving advice and feedback
	• relating back to purpose
Narration	• drawing out relevant features
	• informing future work
The teacher may be	
• narrating as the children are doing the actions	
• narrating while the children are in tableau	**Asking questions**
• narrating in order to set the context for the meeting or ritual about to happen	• negotiating next stages of development
• narrating in order to move the story on to the next stage	• reflecting on own work
• narrating in order to bring a closure to the story or event	• reflecting on actions of roles within the drama
	• reflecting on outcomes
	• speculating on the future

Figure 4.6

strategies that the teacher might use to give the drama structure and to keep the story moving. Those strategies down the left hand side can be used while the drama is up and running and happening in 'now time'. In all the examples used in this chapter, the teacher has taken a role and, to a greater or lesser extent, has entered into the drama with the children. From her role, the teacher can exert influence on its direction and pace. As Figure 4.6 shows, the teacher may be in a high-status role (as the representative from the water company in the reservoir drama, for example), an equal-status role (as one of the villagers in the Saxon drama) or a low-status role (as the pig who is looking for a suitable home). Each of these roles makes different demands of both teacher and children, but all offer opportunities for the teacher to work from inside the drama, demonstrating her commitment to it and allowing her to influence it from within.

At other times the teacher may keep the story alive through narration. As we have demonstrated with a number of examples, this may be used to tell or retell a story which children act out; to move on to the next stage of the story (as in the winds drama); or to bring the drama to a satisfactory conclusion. There are also times when we pause and take time to dwell within certain moments of the story. Such work may well involve rehearsal and performance, whether in the form of still image, ritual or short playlet. In giving such tasks to children, it is important that the brief be as clear as possible. Tight deadlines and clear constraints can generate purposeful action and help children craft their work more carefully. At times, the outcome of these tasks may feed straight into the live drama. In the example where children had to make images and words to represent the different winds, these were brought straight to the 'gathering' and thus maintained their novelty and surprise. In the example of the still images of Saxon life, however, the class reviewed and commented on each group's work and had the opportunity to revise and refine their work before it became part of the whole-class ritual.

Moving the thinking on: teacher questioning in the drama lesson

Most teachers are highly skilled at questioning. Whether they deploy these skills to get to the bottom of a situation in the playground, or to develop children's thinking as they explore complex ideas in science, they well know how to probe understandings, extend thinking and challenge children's responses and assumptions. These same skills can be deployed for similar purposes in a drama lesson.

We have already stressed the value of identifying two or three key questions which serve to give overall purpose and direction to the drama. They are the 'big' questions which the work as a whole will raise and seek to address. As the work progresses, however, the teacher will need continuously to pose specific questions in a variety of contexts and for a range of purposes. Much questioning is done when both teacher and children are out of role and discussing how the drama will progress. In the example of the Saxon drama, the teacher is preparing the class for the discussion or 'talk time' that will follow the ritual. She asks the children, 'What sorts of things do you think the people need to talk about?' As the children respond with answers such as 'How the harvest has been?' or 'How well the animals are doing?' the teacher may probe for deeper answers with questions such as 'Why would they need to talk about that?' or 'Why would that be important to them?' Such questions are intended to encourage the thinking needed to prepare the class so that the eventual meeting makes sense, has purpose and maintains momentum. She also asks questions about the form of the people's meeting: 'Who gets to speak?'; 'How do they decide?'; 'How do they make sure that everyone does not speak at once?' She could, of course, simply tell them how the meeting is going to be: she probably has plenty of ideas of her own about how it could be structured and the sorts of things the people might say. By encouraging the children to think through both the form and content of the meeting it becomes more the product of their own ideas and they are thus being encouraged to take more responsibility for it. This increased responsibility is an important part of children's progression in drama, as we shall see later.

Questioning is also extensively used within the drama when both teacher and children are in role. In the example of the three pigs story, the teacher, in role as the pig, makes constant use of questioning when she is being shown round the exhibition. At each house she asks a range of questions from the factual – 'How many rooms has it got?' – through to more complex questions which encourage the children to think about the implications of their chosen materials – 'What happens if the sun gets too hot and it starts to melt?'

One of the commonest distinctions made is between 'open' and 'closed' questions. Open questions are those which are open to a wide range of responses; closed questions may need only a 'yes' or 'no' answer. In terms of managing the drama it is more helpful to think about a distinction between those questions which open out the drama to a number of possibilities and those which close it down and narrow its focus. Both types of questioning will be appropriate at different stages of the work's development. 'Opening out' questions help to build the story as, for instance, in the discussion about the Saxons' everyday lives. A question such as, 'What do the people of the village do all day?' opens up a range of possible responses, some of which could be inappropriate, of course. In this case, given the work they have already done in the classroom, the teacher would not expect the children to respond that the Saxons spent all day watching television! Later in the drama however, the story may need closing down. When the discussion about what to do in the face of the threatened raid seems to have run its course, the teacher, in role as the traveller, closed the discussion down by saying, 'Time is short. Are you staying or going?' thus reducing the debate to two possible responses: we go or we stay.

Figure 4.7 shows how teachers might think of questions along a continuum from those which open the drama up to those which close in and focus it more tightly. The diagram also separates those which happen outside the drama from those which are asked when the drama is alive, when both children and teacher are in role. Questions at all these levels serve important but differing purposes in extending the children's thinking and keeping the story moving.

This chapter has shown how, with appropriate planning, structuring and management, we can connect drama with many other areas of the curriculum. From the child's point of view this can offer valuable opportunities to place learning in real human contexts by making stories and living through them, rather than hearing them told by the teacher. As active participants in the drama, children can recognise the story which develops as a communal creation, the result of everyone's work. As part of a broad and balanced curriculum, drama has a significant contribution to make.

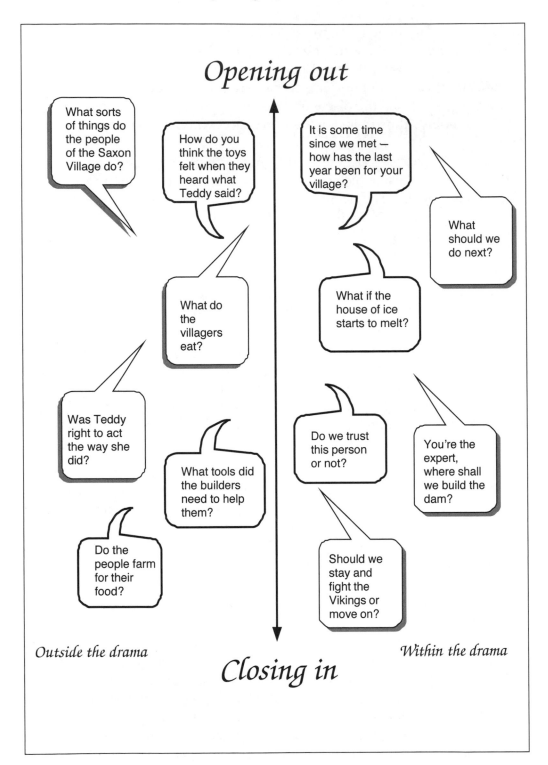

Figure 4.7

Chapter 5

Drama and literacy

In September 1998, the National Literacy Strategy (NLS) was introduced in English primary schools. All schools were expected to establish clear plans and targets for how they would improve children's abilities in the skills of reading and writing. The vast majority of schools have adopted the practice of the daily *literacy hour* and plan their work from the *Framework for Teaching*: a programme of teaching objectives for 4 to 11 year olds. This strong emphasis on the teaching of reading and writing might be seen to make it harder rather than easier for teachers to find time for drama. In this chapter we outline some of the ways in which drama can support the development of literacy both within and beyond a daily literacy lesson.

The *Framework for Teaching* makes a number of explicit references to drama and includes many other teaching objectives which can be supported by using drama as part of your daily practice. As well as specifying teaching objectives for each term of the primary phase, the Framework also sets out the *Range of Work* to be covered: the text types and genres from which examples should be drawn. The range includes a wide variety of fiction, poetry and non-fiction and makes explicit reference to playscripts in each year.

Using drama in the literacy hour

The NLS is founded upon the practice of the daily *literacy hour*. The intention is that regular routines are established in which children meet consistent patterns of teaching as they move through the school. The structure of the daily hour is also intended to maintain a balance of teaching at the levels of the word, the sentence and the text. In the practice of a daily hour teachers need to strike a careful balance between maintaining routines with which children become familiar and sustaining energy and freshness in their approaches. Adopting techniques and strategies from the field of drama can be a very powerful way not only of deepening children's understanding of texts, but also of enlivening and adding variety to the daily approaches.

Shared text work

In this section, the first fifteen minutes of the hour, the whole class focus on a text that they are reading or writing. As we explored in chapter 2, dramatising stories in various ways can make a very important contribution to deepening children's understanding. Some of the strategies we outlined can be used very effectively in the first part of the hour. For example:

- **acting out** a story (using the story stick) encourages children to reflect on the structure of the plot as a whole and summarise the main points;
- **hot-seating** is an excellent way of encouraging children to explore and understand character, drawing on inferences that they can make from their reading of the text;
- **conscience alley** might be used when the class are exploring a difficult decision which a character faces;
- **thought tracking** can be developed by the teacher reading through a section of text and leaving pauses for groups or individuals to speak characters' thoughts and feelings;
- **forum theatre** might be used to explore possible outcomes of a particular moment in a story.

It is important to emphasise that such strategies can make an important contribution to the hour provided that you are clear that they take children *closer* and *more deeply into* the texts which they are reading. Relating the activities to particular objectives set out in the Framework will help to keep this focus clear.

Word level work

For younger children, this section of the hour is dedicated to developing the graphophonic skills which enable them to understand how the sounds of speech are represented as words on the page. NLS materials on phonics set out a number of steps in teaching these skills, many of which are developed through games. Although drama may not be applied directly to the teaching of these skills, it is important to emphasise the essential contribution that speaking and listening make to their development. Step 1 in the NLS materials is concerned with development of general sound discrimination, speech sound discrimination, rhythm and rhyme, and alliteration: all of which are developed through the stories, sounds, songs and rhymes with which teachers who use drama are so familiar. Drama is also a powerful means by which children engage with rich and varied language; engagement which is vital if they are to make the most of the vocabulary extension set out in the word level strand of the Framework.

Sentence level work

In this section of the hour, the class explore and investigate grammar and punctuation. The ways in which writers use grammar will be influenced by their intended audiences and purposes: as we shall show later in this chapter, there are a number of ways in which drama can help children to understand how this is influenced by the *context* of a particular piece of writing. It is also worth noting that individuals often have their own characteristics of grammar: the length of their sentences; the ways in which they construct them; the characteristics of local dialect. As children's writing becomes more sophisticated, handling the ways in which their characters use grammar can be a very important way of developing them for the intended reader. Spoken language, which might be developed through a technique such as hot-seating, can be a very powerful way of exploring and developing such mannerisms before beginning writing.

Group and independent work

During this third section of the hour, children work in groups, sometimes with guidance from their teacher, but often working independently. Some of the activities outlined in chapter 2 might form part of this section, for example: preparing a retelling of a story using puppets; making story maps to explore the setting of a story; working on endings to a story which you have developed earlier. When playscripts are the focus, children may be annotating and preparing a section for performance; writing their own section of script based on a story which they have looked at in shared text work; acting sections of a text and adding stage directions according to the way they want the section performed. In all these activities, actively dramatising text can provide powerful ways of deepening children's understanding either in response to their reading, or as support for their writing.

The plenary

In this last section of the hour the children feed back and discuss what they have learned during the session. Children may have the opportunity to perform short pieces on which they have been working or may use a number of drama techniques to present and explore their findings. For example, they may offer a character for hot-seating a second time, but include additional information and understanding which they have gained from their group and independent work. Groups may present their work in the form of a monologue or soliloquy in which a character speaks about how she or he is feeling at a particular point in a story, or they may present a dramatised reading of a section of text in which different members of the group take different roles from the story.

All of the approaches outlined above indicate how the skills that you and your class develop in drama can be incorporated into your focused teaching of the skills of reading and writing. Such approaches are valid ways of keeping teaching and learning lively, relevant and exciting for children while maintaining a clear focus on the objectives set out in the NLS Framework. The following examples show how you might develop the relationship between drama and literacy more fully.

Example 1: *Dogger* (Year 2)

Dogger, by Shirley Hughes, is a well-established story in the early years. It tells the story of Dave and his favourite toy called Dogger whom he loses – the story centres on the trouble Dave has getting Dogger back. It has a clearly structured plot, readily identifiable characters, and a setting which is familiar to many young children. In the NLS Framework, it fits into the range of work set out in Year 2, Term 1. The Framework specifies that children should be taught to 'be aware of the difference between spoken and written language' (Y2 T1, Text 3) – retelling the story with the 'story stick' as described in Chapter 2 is an ideal way of exploring this idea as well as helping children to 'understand time and sequential relationships in stories' (Y2 T1, Text 4) and 'to identify and discuss reasons for events in stories, linked to plot' (Y2 T1, Text 5).

Having established the overall structure of the plot, use a puppet to take the role of Dogger. You can either control the puppet yourself, or give the opportunity to one or more children: this is a very good way of exploring the 'parallel' story of what happens to Dogger when he is lost. When and where did Dave leave him? How did he end up getting put on the toy stall? Where did he spend the night? How did he feel? Exploring questions such as these not only encourages children to understand the overall structure of the plot, it also encourages them to think about the bits which Shirley Hughes *doesn't* tell, but are none the less there for her readers to infer.

Other characters might also be hot-seated. Mum, Dad, Bella, the woman on the toy stall, Dave himself – each will have their own particular view of events and their own story to tell. This activity can also offer children the opportunity to challenge the versions of events and attitudes of some of the characters. Dave's dad, for instance, might be projected as being annoyed by the whole series of events and thinking that it is time Dave had grown out of Dogger and started playing with more 'grown up' toys – in this way children are encouraged to relate their own experience to the story (Y2 T1, Text 6) and are challenged to explain to Dad why Dogger might be so important to Dave.

One of the key moments in the story – when Dogger has been bought by a little girl – can also be explored by using a simple version of forum theatre. Ask the class to imagine that Bella did not win a big teddy bear in the raffle (in Shirley Hughes's story, Bella swaps this teddy for Dogger), but that Bella and Dave have to find a different way of persuading her to give them Dogger. It is a good idea if the teacher takes the role of the little girl because the children have the job of persuading her – from within the role you can make it as difficult for them as you want, but still know that you will give in in the end! Two children take the roles of Bella and Dave, but they are supported by the rest of the class. The action is played out, but anyone – either the role players or other members of the class – can stop the action to give advice to Bella and Dave about how best to persuade the little girl. They may, of course, suggest some rather brutal ways of persuading the girl to part with Dogger – should this happen, the teacher in role can call for her mum, stop the action, and point out that more gentle and tactful persuasion may be called for! What else could we try?

By examining this one moment in the story in such detail, children develop an insight into the logic or 'grammar' of the story; the way in which events connect to make overall sense. If the girl were to give Dogger up immediately, some of the impact of the story would be lost, but if she held on and refused to let go, the reader would be left with an unsatisfactory ending in which Dave never got Dogger back. Having explored the ending of the story in this way, children can be encouraged to write their own alternative – they know what to write, because they saw it and made it happen.

Example 2: *Arthur* (Year 4)

Arthur, by Amanda Graham and illustrated by Donna Gynell, is the story of an ordinary brown dog. He lives in a pet shop and dearly wants 'a home with a pair of old slippers to chew'. As he notices other animals getting sold, be they rabbits, fish or snakes, Arthur tries to behave like one so that he might find a home of his own. Although this story is also suitable for quite young children, its simple plot, single setting, and wide range of characters make it a good choice to adapt as a play. The Framework suggests that children should 'write playscripts, e.g. using known stories as a basis' (Y4 T1, Text 13).

If children have been following the Framework, they will already have some experience of the major differences in the ways in which plays and prose are written (Y3 T1, Text 5). It is important to revisit these distinctions before work on Arthur begins. Throughout this work, it is essential to stress that plays are not written to be read as novels, or even to be 'read round' in small groups: they are written to be *performed*. What is written down is there to enable a performance: the script isn't the play just as a musical score isn't the music. Only when sound, light, movement, gesture, and all the subtleties of spoken language are added does the play come 'off the page'. As children work on their adaptation of this story, it is important that they keep trying their ideas out *in action*.

One of the advantages of the story is that it has so little dialogue to begin with – it presents a challenge which demands that the children think hard about the story itself and how it might be told in the form of a play, rather than merely identifying dialogue and 'converting' it into a script. Begin by discussing and listing the problems that the story presents. One solution which the children may suggest is the idea of a narrator – someone who fills in the bits of the plot which are not made clear by the action and dialogue. In order to explore the differences between plays and prose fully, it is better to discourage this device.

Before beginning work on the play, it is important to have thoroughly explored and understood the story: this will happen through whole-class shared reading of the text (it is available as a big book), and possibly some guided group work with some of the readers. You can then begin exploring and developing the characters. In Chapter 2, we saw how the Hunter might be presented in different ways: you can use the same idea with the character of Mrs Humber, the pet shop owner. Hot-seat her once and project her as a caring woman who loves all the animals in her shop, then offer a second characterisation in which you show her as a hard-headed business woman who intends to 'dispose' of Arthur if he is not sold soon. It is worth pointing out to the children that both these versions of Mrs Humber are entirely consistent with Amanda Graham's story, even with Donna Gynell's illustration – a powerful illustration of how characters are often created as much by the reader as by the writer. Which version do the children prefer? Which make for a better play? How will their preferred character be developed through the script?

In the next session, begin by devising a list of characters who will be in the play. From their reading of plays, children should already be familiar with the idea of a cast list, even of *dramatis personae*. The characters of Arthur, Mrs Humber, Melanie and her Grandad are all clear from the original story, but the children will quickly realise that it is going to be difficult to tell the story with only these (unless, of course, Arthur has some extremely long monologues!). Once they realise that the story also refers to rabbits, snakes and fish, and that the illustrations show many more animals, possibilities for telling the story differently begin to open up.

Having discussed where it might happen, the first scene can be written as a piece of shared writing. The children might suggest that the opening scene takes place at night when the pet shop is closed. Perhaps Arthur is telling the other animals about his fear that he will never get a home. How do they react? Are they all friendly and helpful or are there some animals who are less than kind? Which will make the play more effective? Once a short section of dialogue is written, it is important to get children up, trying different ways of speaking the lines aloud and adding action so they can see how the play works *in performance* – only then can they make judgements about the effectiveness of their writing.

In the next shared writing session you will need to think about the overall structure of the play. How many scenes will there be and what will happen in each? Once this overall outline has been developed, different groups can be given responsibility for different scenes. It is worth noting however, that unless there has been sufficient shared discussion about the characters and how they will be presented, there is danger of different groups developing them in entirely different ways so that the eventual play will lack coherence. As groups work on their particular scenes, encourage them to keep trying their dialogue out – how does it sound in performance? In the plenary session, groups can present their work, but again, it is important to encourage them to perform it rather than merely read it aloud.

A further session can involve groups annotating each other's sections of script – what is unclear? Is there a need to add stage directions? How much should be left to the interpretation of the performer? Over a number of lessons, the play can be written, revised and edited, all according to how it develops in performance. Having written their play, the children are very likely to want to perform it. Since this work will probably take place in the autumn term and Christmas is a very popular time for performance in the primary school, the whole project could culminate in a production of the finished play using some of the ideas in Chapter 6. Why not offer copies of the script for sale in the foyer afterwards?

Example 3: *Romeo and Juliet* (Year 6)

The Framework suggests the range for Year 6 Term 1 should include 'where appropriate, the study of a Shakespeare play'. With children of this age, it is unlikely that you would expect them to read every word of a play, but they can certainly enjoy exploring short extracts of Shakespeare's language, especially when these are placed within the context of the whole story. Leon Garfield's collection of *Shakespeare Stories* is an excellent resource since he not only gives a clear understanding of the plot of a play, but he makes extensive use of Shakespeare's dialogue in the telling. We recommend that unless you know the play well, you read his version of *Romeo and Juliet* before commencing this work.

Much of this work takes place outside the literacy hour, and you will need a good-sized space – probably the hall. Begin with some 'eye contact' games. For example, the class stand in a circle and you signal to each member of the class to sit down just by establishing eye contact and making some small silent signal (winking, raising an eyebrow etc.). You can then play a different version in which you signal to the first person to sit, but then they signal to the next and so on – everyone has to concentrate and look at the last person to sit because they will be the next to signal.

Next you ask children to work in pairs – they have to move around the space, always maintaining eye contact with their partner. The pairs can then become fours – this time each pair moves around together keeping a constant eye on their 'partner pair'. After experiencing this for a few moments, pause and discuss how it felt – in what kind of a place might this happen? Children will notice that it creates a hard and aggressive atmosphere. Then give each group copies of these lines from Act 1 Scene 1 of the play:

> *Gregory*: I will frown as I pass by, and let them take it as they list.
> *Sampson*: Nay, as they dare. I will bite my thumb at them, which is a disgrace to them, if they bear it.
> *Abraham*: Do you bite your thumb at us, sir?
> *Sampson*: I do bite my thumb, sir.
> *Abraham*: Do you bite your thumb at us, sir?
> *Sampson*: [Aside to Gregory] Is the law of our side if I say ay?
> *Gregory*: No.
> *Sampson*: No, sir, I do not bite my thumb at you, sir; but I bite my thumb, sir.
> *Gregory*: Do you quarrel, sir?
> *Abraham*: Quarrel, sir! No sir.

Read the lines through with the children and explore their meaning, then give them opportunities to read them through in their groups of four – encourage them to get up and try different ways of speaking the lines. It is important to point out that another character, Balthasar, is present in the scene although he does not speak. Suggest that the fourth member of the group takes this role, stands at Abraham's side and perhaps 'echoes' the last couple of words of each of Abraham's lines.

When the groups have had time to rehearse reading these few lines, ask them to separate so that those children playing Abraham and Balthasar are well away from their corresponding Gregory and Sampson. They then walk towards each other, maintaining the eye contact from the original game, and play out the scene once they are close enough. All the groups play the scene simultaneously.

On their next run through, ask the children not to stop at the end of the scene, but to carry on building the developing dispute. They can add words of their own or repeat lines that they have already used, but the dispute must get louder *without* anyone making any physical contact! When the scene has reached a crescendo, the teacher reads this adaptation of the speech by the Prince:

> *Prince*: Rebellious subjects, enemies to peace,
> Profaners of this neighbour-stained steel,
> Will they not hear? What ho, you men, you beasts,
> Throw your mistempered weapons to the ground,
> And hear the sentence of your moved prince.
> Three civil brawls bred of airy word,
> By thee, old Capulet, and Montague,
> Have thrice disturbed the quiet of our streets.
> If ever you disturb our streets again
> Your lives shall pay the forfeit of the peace.
> For this time all the rest depart away:
> You, Capulet, shall go along with me;
> And Montague, come you this afternoon
> To know our farther pleasure in this case,
> To old Freetown, our common judgement-place.
> Once more, on pain of death, all men depart.

It is not necessary for the children to understand the detail of this speech, since you can convey much of the meaning by the tone of your delivery: the Prince is very angry! You may wish to explore the extract in more detail as part of your shared reading at another time, but for now it is enough that the children should know something of the atmosphere at the beginning of the play – the two households at each other's throats and minor disputes always in danger of becoming something more. From this start, you can develop work on the rest of the play.

Divide the class into eight groups and assign each the task of making a still image with one of the following titles:

1. A formal dance
2. A beautiful face is seen at a window
3. A secret wedding
4. A sword fight in which two men are slain
5. Pleading for life
6. Banished for ever
7. Ordered to marry
8. Planning in secret

Having learned the outline of the plot (or perhaps made yourself a few notes from Leon Garfield's telling), you can use the children's still images to help tell the story. Once they know the story, ask two children to represent the figures of the dead Romeo and Juliet. Then invite each of them to join the image in some way which represents their attitude to or feeling about the story they have just heard: they may stand by the dead lovers but turn away; they may kneel as if at prayer; they may just hang heads in sorrow. In this way you can assemble a whole-class still image as a final tableau in the story. Over this image you can read the last lines of the play:

> *Prince*: A glooming peace this morning with it brings.
> The sun, for sorrow will not show his head.
> Go hence, to have more talk of these sad things.
> Some shall be pardon'd, and some punished;
> For never was a story of more woe
> Than this of Juliet and her Romeo.

Using the approach we have outlined, it is possible to cover this work in little over an hour. Obviously, there is potential for much more extended work, but this approach demonstrates how a class can be introduced to and actively engaged with the play in even the most crowded timetable.

Drama and non-fiction

Dramas use stories to explore issues of human significance. This principle, which we have stressed throughout, might suggest that there is little potential for supporting the reading and writing of non-fiction through drama. Yet to be effective readers and writers of non-fiction, children need to understand and be familiar with the *context* of the work: why is it written? For whom? What is its intended purpose? Many teachers will try to overcome this problem by choosing examples from real contexts: letters to the local paper on local issues; advertisements for products with which children are familiar; non-fiction related to other areas of the curriculum that children are studying. Selecting texts like this is an excellent way of making them relevant for children and helping them understand how the social context of non-fiction writing determines both the content (what is written) and the form (the way in which it is written). However, it is not always possible to find these 'real' contexts, particularly when the Framework sets out so clearly the stages at which particular non-fiction text types are to be studied. As the following examples demonstrate, by working with drama, it becomes possible to create *fictional contexts* for reading and writing non-fiction.

Non-fiction and imaginative play

In Chapter 3 we outlined a model for planning imaginative play areas in the early years. Each of the contexts suggested offers many opportunities for reading and writing non-fiction. Health centres, for instance, are full of texts including leaflets and posters giving advice, notices giving information about times of clinics, and information about where patients can get help. As well as collecting real examples of such texts to put in the health centre, a context like this offers countless opportunities for children to experiment with writing them. It is important that the need for these texts is generated by the *story* of the health centre: the teacher may introduce the idea that there have been a lot of cases of stomach upset recently and perhaps they should put some posters up about food hygiene. A poster or leaflet might be written during shared writing in the literacy hour, but because the children understand the context, they will find it much easier to understand how it is written and why. Each example we gave in Chapter 3 will offer many possibilities of its own, some initiated by the children, others suggested by adults.

Reading in role

It is often easier for children to be genuinely and constructively critical of non-fiction if they are given a role (or 'frame') from which to read it. If, for example, you are looking at advertising, you might ask the class to imagine that they are the board of a company who have commissioned a campaign for one of their products. You take the role of a representative of the advertising firm and bring a draft of your advert – it might be cut from a real newspaper or magazine, or you may use a fictional example from published materials you use to support your work in literacy. It is important that the roles you have given the children are powerful, expert and critical – in the fictional context of the advert you have much lower status than they do and this will encourage a much more critical reading of the text than they might be prepared to offer in the course of normal classroom discussion. Asking children to read something 'as if we were...' is a strategy you can use regularly in both literacy and drama teaching.

Non-fiction as part of extended drama work

In Chapter 4 we looked at a number of examples illustrating how drama might relate to the rest of the primary curriculum. Example 4 (p. 59) describes a project undertaken by a Year 5 class, which looked at the building of a reservoir and its impact on the local community. Work such as this offers plenty of opportunities for linking work in the literacy hour. The NLS Range of Work for Year 5 includes:

- persuasive writing to put or argue a point of view: letters, commentaries, leaflets to persuade, criticise, protest, support, object, complain.

Examples of these forms of writing will be used as shared texts during your work in the literacy hour, helping children to understand the ways in which such texts are structured and the language features which characterise them. When you ask them to write their own, children are helped by their thorough knowledge not only of the form and style of such writing, but also of the context for which they are writing it. They are also presented with challenges from a number of viewpoints. When you write the letter inviting residents to the meeting (which might be done as shared writing), children see it from the point of view of the water company, but later on in the drama they are asked to read and react to this letter as the residents of the area that will be affected. As the story develops, the residents may wish to write letters of protest, objection, or complaint: skills which you can develop further through your planned literacy teaching.

By linking these forms of writing to the story of the reservoir, children have a much clearer understanding of how both form and content are determined by the context in which they are written. Though we are dealing with *non-fiction texts*, their *fictional contexts* can make them much more relevant and accessible for children.

Chapter 6

Drama, community and performance in the primary school

Performance is central to drama. In the classroom dramas described in previous chapters children were given the opportunities to shape, rehearse and present dramatic material, make use of space, objects, time and presence, as well as watch and comment upon each other's work. Characteristically, this kind of performance is developed and shared by the community of the classroom alone. It is not meant for other audiences, nor would it normally serve any useful purpose to go through the lengthy production processes necessary to make of it a valid dramatic experience for such an audience. However, such drama productions do have a significant role to play within primary schools, in both educational and cultural terms, and it is to this kind of performance, intended for a public beyond the immediate classroom, that we shall now turn our attention.

A school is a community and performances of various kinds – assemblies, religious festivals, concerts, plays – serve to bring members of a community together to articulate and celebrate the values they share. Many schools recognise and value the important contribution drama can make in helping to foster and build a sense of communal identity, and drama features regularly in school assemblies, religious celebrations such as Christmas and Diwali, and end-of-term productions. It is performances such as these that can attract the attention of the wider community of families, school governors and ancillary staff and they can do a great deal to enhance a school's standing within its local area. For the children who take part in such productions, the challenges can be great – of commitment, concentration and teamwork – but the successful negotiation of these challenges can contribute towards a significant sense of communal achievement. This sense of belonging, of group identity that performance can help engender, is one of the key ways in which drama can contribute towards children's social and moral development.

The emphasis on community is, therefore, an important one and it can be enhanced by the theatrical model you adopt when working towards a production. We believe that an *ensemble* approach to devising and performing is especially appropriate to primary schools. In this process, groups discuss and work through ideas together, creating theatre as a living text with scripts tending to emerge from rather than predetermine the making of the drama. Such a model for devising texts is very adaptable to time, space, the numbers involved in the production and the particular talents of individuals, whereas most playtexts will tend to set these requirements in advance, regardless, of course, of particular contextual considerations. Within performance, such a model removes the star category, once again emphasising group work and partnership, placing complementary demands upon the performers rather than offering great challenges to the few and very little to challenge the many. Such a model can be fluid, with characters being played collectively, individual performers moving between chorus figures and main characters, and meanings being made as much through physical shape, sound, music and movement as through speech. Its adaptability therefore allows for other performing art forms such as dance and music to be easily incorporated within the final performance text, thus presenting a broader platform of opportunities for children who may be physically rather than verbally expressive. There is an evident connection between such a flexible model for performance and the approach to classroom drama we have described in previous chapters.

Schools sometimes offer valuable extra-curricular time for drama in the form of drama clubs, which can be either performance or non-performance oriented. The two examples of small-scale performance described below are offered as possible models of ensemble theatre for primary school children. They could be adapted and worked on within such an extra-curricular framework but we have chosen them because they were conceived and developed as whole-class projects, largely within curriculum time, with some additional use of extra-curricular hours. The overall model presents opportunities for you to link with other curriculum areas, most noticeably music and dance but also English, where you could develop script work and explore the stories through discussion, writing and further reading; the spiritual, social and moral curriculum, where some of the questions and themes at the heart of the dramas could be explored in more generalised terms; and information and computer technology for management of sound and light and for other communications including ticket and programme design. As well as embracing the principles inherent to ensemble theatre, the projects are flexible enough for aspects to be worked upon and staged as a class or year-group assembly.

Example 1: *The Enchanter's Daughter* (Year 6)

This tale by Antonia Barber, illustrated by Erroll le Cain and published by Red Fox, tells of a powerful Enchanter who lives alone with his Daughter in a cold white land, high on the top of a mountain. The Daughter has never known the world beyond the palace, knows of no other life outside its walls and has no name. The events of the story are set during her adolescence, as she grows lonely and restless and increasingly estranged from her father. Wishing to spend more and more time with his books in order to discover the magic that will help him conquer death, the Enchanter conjures up story books for his Daughter to occupy her time so that she will leave him in peace. But in these books, she discovers that there exist lands outside the palace, lands inhabited by many different people, all of whom have names; and that children have mothers as well as fathers. She returns to the Enchanter but he refuses to tell her her name or her origin. Instead he attempts to trick her into believing that she never had a mother and was conjured by him from a rose. She pleads with him to let her spend one more day as a rose and this he agrees to; but the experience convinces her that she never was a rose, and subsequent transformations into a fish and a fawn leave her with the same conviction. Realising that the Enchanter will never tell her the truth, she plots her escape and asks to be transformed into an eagle; but the Enchanter smiles and tells her she was never an eagle, only a 'pretty flying bird'. As such a bird, she flies over the palace walls and across the mountains and forests but, after a day's painful flight the spell wears off and, transforming back into human form, she falls from the sky. Found by a mountain shepherd who carries her back to the farm he shares with his mother, the Daughter recovers consciousness in the presence of an old woman who is weeping as she nurses her. The woman explains that she reminds her of the daughter she lost many years before. A rich merchant had stopped by and, amused by the little girl, had offered to buy her. The offer had been refused but the very next day the girl had disappeared without trace. The Daughter, sensing that this is her story, asks the name of the girl; it is 'Thi-Phi-Yen' which indeed means 'Pretty Flying Bird'. The Enchanter's Daughter has found her true identity, her true mother and her true home.

The story, therefore, creates an appealing world of fantasy and magic to explore symbolically issues of identity, parent–child relationships, the nature of power and the inevitability of death. It also uses established fairy tale motifs in ways which challenge those of more traditional tales. For example, we have a wicked stepfather rather than a stepmother and the heroine's happiness is achieved through a journey away from the material wealth of a princess rather than towards it. These themes integral to the tale can all be explored in detail within other curriculum areas. The details below are

restricted to the drama work, which was largely developed over a full term
for an hour a week in the hall, and is presented in two parts. The initial
activities encourage children to explore the story's themes through drama
and allow them to develop and play with its narrative possibilities before
hearing the story itself. The devising process which follows builds upon this
initial work whilst developing new material specifically for performance.

Exploring the story

1. The children sit in a circle. All say their name in turn and are invited to
   offer any history behind them – do they know why they were given
   their names? Are they aware of their origins, meanings or of any famous
   people from history or in stories who shared their name?
2. The teacher, in role as the Enchanter's Daughter, introduces the children
   to her plight:

'I am the Enchanter's Daughter. I live here, with my father, the Enchanter,
in a palace at the top of the world. He calls me Daughter, I call him Father
– there are no names in this palace and I have never journeyed beyond its
walls. When I was younger, he used to play with me but now he just pores
over his books in his room at the top of the tower. One day I tried to see
what it was that engrossed him so but, for the first time ever, he grew angry
with me. Then, with a wave of his arm through the air, he told me to return
to my room where I would find my own books – story books – and I did.
And in them I found out about the many lands that exist beyond the
mountains surrounding the palace; that there are sons as well as daughters,
mothers as well as fathers. And that each and every one of them has a name.
And I want to find my mother and I need to know my name.'

3. Out of role, the teacher invites the children to speculate upon her
   situation, upon what they know and do not know about the Daughter.
   Then the teacher re-enters the role and informs the children that she is
   seated in the centre of a room of mirrors and that each of them is her
   reflection and has the power to question her if they wish. They can also
   advise her upon how she might go about finding out from the Enchanter
   the truth of her own and her mother's identity. The teacher uses the
   original story to inform the answers she gives in role.
4. The children are informed that the Daughter has decided to go and
   question the Enchanter the following morning to try and find out all
   she can. She then has a dream in which she steals into his room and
   peers into his book of spells, one of which fills her with dread, the
   other with hope. Children are invited to speculate as to what these
   spells might have been. Using still images, each group creates a picture
   from the book depicting the result of one such spell. They then invent

the words of the spell and chant these words as they form the images. These are viewed in turn.

5. The children organise the space to represent the room in the Enchanter's tower. In **collective role**, four or five of them play the Enchanter, the rest of the class the Daughter. Before the role-play begins, the teacher quietly instructs the Enchanter to provide answers which avoid telling the Daughter what she wants to know. This helps the children sustain the necessary tension by ensuring that the role-play focuses on the strained relationship between the two rather than on issues of plot. During the role-play the teacher remains as a side coach, contributing to either voice as and when helpful.

6. The children discuss the stalemate that has resulted from the discussion and speculate upon the possible courses of action now open to the Daughter, in particular, how she might make her escape from the Enchanter.

7. The teacher switches the focus to a woman who lives beyond the mountains. In role, she sits holding a doll and explains how she has just found it in an old trunk, that it has made her sad as it reminds her of the Daughter she once had but whom she lost long ago. The children are then invited to identify the woman as the Daughter's mother, who is then hot-seated as the teacher in role.

8. The children now speculate as to how the Mother and Daughter might be reunited. In groups they are to devise an ending for the story with the following principles of fairy tale structure being observed:

- there must be magic;
- the Daughter must make a journey;
- the final 'obligatory' scene must present us with the Daughter's name and inform us as to how she came to be separated from her mother.

These can be refined and presented in the form of a very short playlet.

9. Children observe and discuss the various endings. It is only at this point that they are shown the book and invited to listen to the original story.

The story in performance

The performance structure offered below is only a framework but, as such, it is flexible and adaptable and will allow you to offer varying amounts of responsibility to the children, according to their capabilities and their previous experience of drama. As a framework for a text rather than a complete, written script, it means that both you and the children will need to construct much of it for yourselves and, in so doing, you can draw freely from the original story as well as from the versions created by the children.

The performance requires a large, level space, such as is normally found in a school hall. Lighting will help but is not essential. Costume can be kept very simple, each child wearing black leggings, perhaps, and a different coloured, plain T-shirt.

Description of performance

A group of children in a corner of the space play a simple piece of music using an electronic keyboard, tuned and untuned percussion and recorders. Children enter the space in turn, each saying their name, some adding a few words to explain its significance or origin. They gather in groups of six or seven and freeze.

A short NARRATIVE LINK introduces the drama. 'We all have names. It is hard to imagine life without a name. Our story tells of a beautiful princess who had no name and of the discoveries she made in her search to find it.'

The groups perform shapes in sequence, each representing the Enchanter's palace on the top of a mountain. Each is introduced by the cymbal and accompanied by a voice/sound collage performed by children grouped at the side of the space. A child runs around and between each in turn, waving a swirling length of white silk to represent the clouds and mountain mist.

Notes on the process

The music links with AT1 'Performing and Composing' in the National Curriculum for music in England. Musicians will join in many of the subsequent, non-musical activities, leaving their instruments in the space and returning to them when necessary.

This and subsequent narrative links can be scripted by the teacher in partnership with the children near the end of the devising process. They serve to ensure that the story's narrative remains coherent. Their performance can be shared among the children and sometimes be accompanied by the opening melody.

The shapes have been inspired by the striking illustration on the first page of the book. There is an evident connection with the National Curriculum for dance. The sound collages have been created from sounds associated with wind blowing on a mountain top and from phrases taken from the opening pages of the story.

A short NARRATIVE LINK introduces the next image, beginning with the words: 'In a palace on the roof of the world lived a powerful Enchanter with his beautiful daughter ...'

A child performs the role of the Enchanter, draped in a cloth and holding a staff. He tells us of his powers, chanting magic spells, and each time he waves his staff, the cymbal crashes and children transform into images to represent the spells.

These spells are taken from those created by the children in section 4 (p. 90).

The groups break and all the children form a circle around one child who wears an item of costume (shawl? scarf?) to identify her as the Enchanter's Daughter. A version of the introductory monologue first spoken by the teacher is now performed by the Daughter. She concludes by referring to a recurring dream in which she walks the endless corridors of the palace, as if in a trap.

The Daughter and the Enchanter can be played by different children in each scene, using items of costume to identify them. The children can also work on agreed gestures, posture and tone of voice.

The image dissolves and children in groups of three perform the dream through a sequence of physical images depicting entrapment with a long, coloured length of cloth. They are performed to taped music which helps create an eerie, dream-like atmosphere.

These have been developed by children playing with a number of such images, then being asked to choose three which vary in level and direction and to link them through movement.

NARRATIVE LINK: 'One morning the Enchanter's Daughter awoke from the dream and, despite her fear, decided to go and see the Enchanter to find out why she had no name and why she had no mother ...'

Two children, downstage in the centre of the space, present a tableau of the Enchanter and the Daughter in the Enchanter's tower. The class then divides in half and groups as **alter-egos** in the space to the side of each character. A dialogue between the Enchanter and his Daughter ensues, with each line being spoken by one of the character's alter-egos. As they perform their lines, each child steps forward and presents a gesture to accompany it. This gesture is held frozen until the scene ends.

The dialogue has been scripted by the teacher but draws from both the book and the role-play created in section 5 (p. 91). It has been written in marker pen on a large piece of paper, with each line numbered. The children have read it through together before it has been cut up and individual lines shared for them to read, repeat and learn. The dialogue ends on a suitably dramatic note which highlights the Daughter's frustration but also her determination.

NARRATIVE LINK: 'That night, as the Enchanter slept, the Daughter crept into the tower. She knew that within the power of his magic lay the chance for her to escape. She opened the book and studied the spells within its covers ...'

One child plays the Daughter, walking through the space, holding the book of spells. As she turns the pages, children perform images of the spells in sequence across the space. The final spell transforms her into a bird and is enacted to a crescendo of vocal and percussive sound.

These spells can be repeated from the earlier depiction of the Enchanter's powers. Alternatively, they could represent the different transformations (a rose, a fish, a fawn) that she undergoes in the original story.

The teacher has discussed with the children whether to use the means of escape suggested by the book. This they have agreed to as they are excited by the possibilities of enacting her flight.

The Daughter's flight over the mountains and through the forest is enacted by a child running through space, waving a large 'flag' of coloured silk attached to the end of a bamboo cane, performed to a mixture of narration and taped music. The narration describes her journey and groups of children create with their bodies the mountains, forests, streams and waterfalls she crosses on her way.

The running with the flag is a high-status role and needs discipline and practice. It is also a lovely experience which all children deserve to try. The teacher has ensured that, over the devising process, all children have had a chance to play with the flag. Different children perform the task each time the play is presented.

The image of the Daughter's flight ends abruptly. Children disperse, the theme tune resumes and a brief narrative link introduces a child in role as the mother, holding a doll. Children group behind her and hum gently as she performs a short monologue.

The monologue has been scripted by a child from section 7 (p. 91).

One of the endings devised by the children has been adapted to form the basis for a conclusion to the drama. Its scripting has been guided by the teacher to fit with the performance conventions of the piece as a whole.

This has been chosen after some discussion with the class for the quality of its ideas and of the performance seen in Section 9 (p. 91).

The performance ends with celebratory singing and dancing. When this stops, children recreate the opening images of the Enchanter's palace, with the Enchanter among them and the sound of the wind whistling about the mountain. A brief piece of narrative speculates on his fate and, slowly and in silence, the images collapse to the floor.

The music and lyrics for the song have been composed and arranged largely by a group of committed children who worked over lunch times. The music coordinator offered help and support.

Example 2: *The Snow Queen* (Year 2)

This well-known fairy tale by Hans Andersen was used by a teacher as the basis of a short performance project over one half term. It was a fully integrated topic combining work in drama, dance, music, English and the visual arts and was completed almost entirely within the curriculum time devoted to these subjects. Some extra hall time was needed in the final few days before the performance. The brief notes below sketch those scenes performed through dance and drama. As with *The Enchanter's Daughter*, the scenes were connected by narrative storytelling, in this case performed mainly through the verses of a song, developed with the support of the music coordinator and sung by all of the children. Some of the music was created

and recorded within music lessons with additional music taken from Vangelis'
Antartica. The children wore simple costumes of white, pale blue or purple
clothing.

Description of performance

The opening verses of the song
introduce Gerda and Kaye's relationship and the shattering of the mirror.

The performance opens with
children grouped in still images
depicting the friendship between
Gerda and Kaye

Children perform the shattering of
the mirror. Pairs of children mirror
each other with slow movements.
Suddenly a cymbal crashes and
they freeze. As the cymbal crashes
repeatedly they continue to freeze
in different jagged shapes. A sound
collage begins, using words such as
'splinter', 'shatter', 'crack', 'smash',
growing louder as it repeats until
the children break away from their
partners. They group in fives in
threatening shapes, facing the
audience while the words are
repeated at full volume. Suddenly
there is silence. The sound of wind
is heard and the children glide
offstage, as if blown by the wind.

Notes on the process

*These have been developed from the
children's ideas and create images
of boys and girls playing together.*

*The initial movement work is clearly
developed from the mirroring
exercise in Chapter 1. The language
work was developed in class time
and used to create visual poems
and explore onomatopoeia.*

The song resumes. We hear that Gerda and Kaye are playing in the snow and a group of children act out activities such as snowballing and tobogganning. The song informs us that a piece of the mirror enters Kaye's eye and we hear one boy scream and see him clutch his face. The song and the activities cease abruptly, children gather around Kaye but he is rude, shouts at them to leave him alone. This they do, with Gerda leaving him last of all.

The depiction of the games was developed from ideas initially improvised but the final work has since been carefully crafted and choreographed under the direction of the teacher.

Kaye lies down and the song informs us that he is sleeping as a snowstorm approaches. Some children now perform a snow dance, gliding like snowflakes, changing pace and levels, gathering together in drifts, moving threateningly towards Kaye, backing away as he appears to awaken. Among them dances the Snow Queen, spinning in her cloak. She and the snowflakes finally group above Kaye and re-form in the shape of a giant sleigh, being driven by the Snow Queen with Kaye alongside her. The song informs us that she is taking him to the Ice Palace, her home.

Children have studied the shapes and symmetries of snow crystals as part of their maths and this study informs the shapes they use. Their movements are informed by words such as float, glide, etc. The music has been created with the support of the music coordinator and consists largely of pitched and unpitched percussion and voice collage. The Snow Queen's cloak has been made from a sheet, designed by the children, sewn by a parent. Its pattern has been formed by children cutting symmetrical snowflake patterns from folded paper, pinning them to the cloak as templates over which they have then blown blue and purple inks through diffusers.

Gerda's journey to find Kaye is presented as a series of still images. The narrative is here spoken as choral speech, with musical sound effects suggesting the river, the horse's hooves, the blizzard, etc.

These images have been initially developed during the children's classwork, where they have worked on the story, using some of the strategies offered in Chapter 2. The narrative was scripted by the teacher in response to the images the children crafted.

The song briefly resumes and its narrative informs us that Gerda has reached the Ice Palace. Children form a large group shape and, using white netting and white streamers of tape, they create arches and corridors under which and along which Gerda must search for Kaye. This is performed to taped music.

The teacher has used the game 'The Magician and the Maze' described in Chapter 1 to allow the Snow Queen to control the maze. As she points with her wand, a cymbal crashes and the corridors change direction, thus making Gerda's search more difficult.

The climax is reached when Gerda, now at one side of the space, sees Kaye, still and frozen at the other, and calls out his name. A word collage begins, softly, then growing louder as she slowly walks through the barrier of netting and streamers held up by the children. Phrases such as 'Ice cold/Snow Queen' compete with 'warm heart/Gerda'. When Gerda reaches Kaye, there is silence as she slowly reaches out her hand and takes his. When Kaye finally utters her name, 'Gerda?' the Snow Queen screams and the Ice Palace collapses.

This is a changed and much simplified version of the story's climax that the teacher has invented. Her intention has been to achieve a dramatic climax that the children could manage and that fits with the conventions of this particular drama. The children are aware of the differences from the original story, which the teacher has read to them in class. The teacher has also displayed different versions of the story in the book corner, encouraging individual children to read them for themselves.

The song resumes and concludes the story on a note of celebration. The images of the children playing happily in the snow are re-formed around Gerda and Kaye, who hold hands. Then all the children hold hands as the final verse is repeated.

Some guidelines for those new to running school drama productions

1. Always discuss and agree a performance project with the management team – the Head, Deputy, Phase or Year Leader – before planning and embarking upon it. Make sure other teachers within the school are informed about it at a staff meeting.

2. Ensure that you disrupt the work of other teachers as little as possible. The hall can be a very busy space, both inside and outside curriculum hours. You will need extra hall-time as the performance approaches. Try to timetable any extra rehearsal time well in advance.

3. Organise at the beginning of the project any additional help you are going to need, whether with technicals, costumes, music or simply supervising the children in a classroom immediately before the performance. Many teachers and ancillary staff will be happy to provide assistance. A letter to parents requesting lengths of material, old sheets, specific items of costume, etc. can be very fruitful.

4. Keep a production notebook in which you note who has offered help, regularly update needs, make notes about particular scenes, etc.

5. Be prepared to give up many lunch hours for the duration of the project and use them for working with small groups of children on specific scenes. Some of this work might be possible in a smaller space than the hall.

6. Always supervise any extra-curricular rehearsals. Check health and safety procedures concerning fire precautions, seating and hall capacity for the performance itself.

7. Educate children into having high standards of respect for their own and one another's work and teach them sound performance discipline. Have high but realistic production values. You will probably get stressful as the production approaches so, if possible, have support staff with you during the final rehearsals.

8. Make good use of the school video recorder. This can not only record the performance for posterity but also assist with assessment when the production is built into the curriculum. It can be used to help children observe their own work in progress and stimulate suggestions as to how they can improve upon it. It can also help capture work on scenes that are going to be left for a few weeks while other scenes are tackled.

9. Have each child write a personal letter of invitation to members of the school governing body and to ancillary staff including school secretaries,

dinner ladies, classroom support, cleaners and cooks. Children can study examples of publicity posters and make their own for display around the school.

10. Keep props and costumes in labelled plastic crates. Older children can be made individually responsible for certain items to be taken from the boxes and placed where necessary and to be returned to the correct box after rehearsal and performance. If you do this, make a note of individual responsibilities next to each child's name.

11. Take photographs and mount a display illustrating the production process when it has finished. Include as part of this children's own writing, contributions to scriptwork, etc. If possible, ask to mount this in the entrance of the school, thus helping drama maintain a high profile and become a visible and valued part of the curriculum.

12. When working with script, have children learn their lines as early as possible. There is a danger in pre-scripted drama of the words being relied upon to carry all the meaning, which is particularly difficult for young children. Working with scripts is a lot more complex than simply 'blocking' the children into suitable stage positions and asking them to speak up. Books which present some good ideas for working towards performance from scripted plays in primary schools are suggested in the bibliography.

Chapter 7

Progression, continuity and assessment in primary drama

The issue of progression will be of central concern to any school attempting to design a drama curriculum. Without an agreed framework to chart how children get better at drama, you and your colleagues will find it difficult to plan for such progression over the medium and long term. A framework for progression should therefore provide guidelines in a number of key areas. First and foremost, it should offer a vision of what it means for children to make progress in drama, explaining the skills and knowledge they require and the kinds of experience they need in order to develop them. Such a vision will be of little use unless it can feed directly into your planning. A policy on progression therefore needs to indicate where in the school's curriculum – in which year groups and in relation to which other curriculum areas – you might plan for specific kinds of drama work. This kind of framework will help you decide what you need to teach in order to extend children's skills and knowledge and lead them into more enriching ways of working. It will thus avoid the problems of too much or too little challenge in the work that you plan. To do this effectively, you will need to know what children have already learned as well as knowing where you need to take them. Hence the reason why the words 'progression' and 'continuity' are so often voiced in the same breath; the one depends upon the other.

If you attempt to draw up a framework for progression within your school, however, you will be faced with a number of difficulties. There are no agreed national guidelines to inform you. Some teachers in your school may not value drama, or they may value it for its ability to develop creativity or the imagination, seeing such qualities as worthwhile in themselves and resistant to easy models of linear progression. As we pointed out in Chapter 4, drama draws its content from areas often associated with English and the humanities. If it is taught as part of cross-curricular topic work, it may be valued as a methodology to develop children's learning in other curriculum areas rather than as a subject in its own right. In such a curriculum model, progression in drama may well be seen as a marginal consideration. Finally, as they are being asked to concentrate increasingly on the 'basics' of literacy and numeracy, teachers may be unwilling to take on the added burden of charting and planning for progression in drama.

While recognising these difficulties, this chapter will address directly those of you, whether specialists or non-specialists, who value drama and who realise that the issues of progression and continuity are too important to be set aside. At the same time, we wish to present you with guidance that is realistic, workable and supportive of good primary practice. Our aim is to establish some principles and to offer some models to help you draw up your own framework for progression, one that will suit the school where you teach. We begin by proposing some underlying principles of progression for the long and short term. We then move on to consider how existing documentation relating to two curriculum areas – personal, social and moral education and English – might help you begin to construct a model for progression in drama within your school. In turning our attention to the areas of drama that make it distinctive from other subjects, we draw once again on existing documentation to propose a framework with its own areas of attainment, end of Key Stage Statements and a table of guidelines with examples to show how the principles we propose might look in practice. We conclude the chapter by addressing the issue of assessment and offer a range of methods to help you systematically assess children's progress in drama without adding too much to your existing workload.

First principles of progression

In the National Curriculum Council's publication *The Arts 5–16*, four principles of progression were proposed. We accept these as sound and list them below, offering our own explanations specific to drama alongside each:

1. *Complexity:* meaning that issues dealt with by younger children can be revisited in more complex and sophisticated ways by more mature children.
2. *Control:* meaning that children should acquire increasing control of the means of dramatic expression and the forms it can take.
3. *Depth:* meaning that children should move progressively as they mature from receiving a broad range of drama experiences to exploring individual projects in more depth.
4. *Independence:* meaning that children should become increasingly autonomous, capable of making and articulating their own judgements with regard to their drama work.

In order to be fully effective these four principles will need to inform long-term planning in a fully implemented, whole-school policy. However, with or without such a policy in place, you will be faced with the day-to-day reality of a given group of children. In the short and medium term, your immediate task is to do three things:

- *match* particular groups of children to levels of work appropriate to their capabilities;
- *motivate* these children to produce work of high quality;
- *move on* to work that builds upon the skills and understandings now acquired.

If the four long-term principles should guide whole-school planning, these three short-term principles – match, motivate and move on – should inform short- and medium-term planning for your particular class or year group. They serve as a reminder that progression is a necessary consideration, not only for termly or half-termly units of work but also for individual lesson plans. Hence the importance of having for each lesson clear learning outcomes of the kind referred to in previous chapters.

Progression and continuity in drama within the personal, social and moral curriculum

Learning in drama is often understood to develop such qualities as empathy, self-confidence, self-control, respect and tolerance for others, the ability to concentrate, to listen and to work constructively in groups. Some specialist drama teachers have reacted against this close identification between drama and the personal, social and moral curriculum as none of these qualities are or should be specific to drama. As general educational aims, it is argued, they should not be seen as the prerogative of drama, which has its own learning agenda located within its artistic and cultural practices. While accepting this, the fact remains that drama is a *social* art form, with the result that young children cannot engage in it without engaging, to a greater or lesser extent, with the kind of personal and social skills listed above. There is therefore a dual relationship between drama and such skills, which are prerequisites *for* drama as well as being exercised *in* drama. Because the successful enjoyment of drama depends upon the practice and use of these skills, drama can be an exceptionally effective platform for children to develop them through experience. The younger the children within the primary years, the more likely it is that personal and social skills will be justifiably uppermost in a teacher's mind when planning for drama. In doing so, she is laying the necessary groundwork for more complex and autonomous work in Key Stages 2 and 3.

Personal and social skills and attitudes are difficult to map progressively but national guidance is available in England in such documents as *Early Learning Goals* (QCA 1999a) and the *Framework for personal, social and health education and citizenship at Key Stages 1 and 2* in the revised *National Curriculum 2000*. In addition, individual schools will offer their own guidance in policies for the spiritual, moral, social and cultural education of their children. Every school will have within its aims statement a vision of the kind of qualities it wishes to promote within its children but an effective PSE policy will also provide examples of how they can be promoted in ways appropriate to different year groups. How such documentation can guide teachers into planning drama activities related to particular age groups is illustrated below, with examples relating to work with children in the early years.

Learning goal/guidelines	Source	Examples
'By the end of the reception year, most children will work as part of a group or class, taking turns and sharing fairly, understanding that there need to be … agreed codes of behaviour.'	Early Learning Goals, p. 23	Various games in Chapter 1 such as *Beans* and *Pass the Tambourine*
'By the end of the reception year, most children will … be sensitive to the needs, views and feelings of others.'	Early Learning Goals, p. 23	The children explore ways of helping the sick old woman in the café drama
KS1 'there are different types of teasing and bullying, that bullying is wrong.'	PSHE 4e	Children learn that the girl's unhappiness at school is because she is being bullied and they act to remedy this (Teddy drama, Chapter 3)
KS2 'there are different kinds of responsibilities, rights and duties … in the community and these can sometimes conflict with each other.'	PSHE 2d	The meeting of the animals of the forest, discussing whether the Forest Child should be allowed to stay (Chapter 2)

As children mature, the personal and social skills they develop within drama should become more closely associated with the demands and requirements of the form itself, in particular those which develop their autonomy and independence. So, for example, a child involved in a school production in Year 6 may well be required to show up regularly during lunch times and after school; learn lines; remember physical moves and motifs; ensure that properties are placed in the right place before a performance; and remain still and silent for substantial periods of time. Such a child will need to show reliability, patience, self-discipline, thoughtfulness, commitment to a group and consideration for other members of that group. Such concrete demands made by drama can be considerable but also considerably rewarding when they come to fruition – hence the potential force of the learning experience.

The examples highlighted on page 104 also illustrate the fact that, as dramas are always *about* something, they explore content as well as develop skills. It is in this area, as we saw in Chapter 4, that drama can draw from the content of subjects such as history, geography and RE while adding a clearly moral dimension to the study. Many of the examples given in that chapter investigated key questions which were clearly of this type:

- Can we always rely on people to give us the information we really want? (Year 3)
- How do communities deal with those who do not conform? (Year 4)
- How do the 'virtues' of the Trojans compare with ours? (Year 6)

Good drama often pivots around such difficult issues of human significance and, when it works, engages both thought *and* feeling. It is natural, therefore, that it should provide a space in the curriculum for moral education, where many of the issues are felt as much as they are reasoned about. The issues will become progressively more complex as children mature – complexity of issue being one of the principles of progression we have defined above. So, for example, the children in Year 1 explore within their play how they can help a sick old woman, whereas those in Year 6 begin to reflect upon the nature of moral behaviour with relation to the concept of the virtues. If you have responsibility for drama in your school, you could coordinate these issues with reference to your established schemes of work. In England, further guidance for particular year groups can be found in national documents such as the *Model syllabuses for Religious Education* (SCAA 1994) and the Citizenship Foundation's publication *You, Me, Us* (1994).

Progression and continuity in drama within the English curriculum

A link between drama and English is firmly established in some countries as 'Language Arts' and has been made statutory in England within the English National Curriculum guidelines. Although the details in the latter are sketchy, the references to drama clearly indicate its importance within the areas of speaking, listening, reading and writing. Reference to the Programmes of Study for Speaking and Listening can help inform you whether your drama work is allowing for a suitable range of opportunity and appropriate challenge within these areas. You may like to consider how far the variety of activities suggested in Chapter 2 can be seen to provide children with the opportunities specified for drama at Key Stage 2, cited below:

Pupils should be taught to:
a) create, adapt and sustain different roles, individually and in groups;
b) use character, action and narrative to convey story, themes, emotions, ideas in plays they devise and script;
c) use dramatic techniques to explore characters and issues (for example hot-seating, flashback);
d) evaluate how they and others have contributed to the overall effectiveness of performances.

One of the key features of drama, as we have seen, is its use of story. In England extra guidance to help you plan for progression in children's understanding of story structure at Key Stages 1 and 2 is included in the programme of teaching objectives for the National Literacy Strategy. Here, precise objectives are listed for each year group, many of which could clearly be applied to children's work in drama, as the following examples illustrate:

Year group	Teaching objective	Example
Y1	To identify and discuss characters, e.g. appearance, behaviour, qualities, and speculate how they might behave	The children discuss their impressions of the Teddy and and the girl who owns it (Chapter 3)

Y2	To discuss and map out simple story plots	Children make a map of the story of *The Forest Child* (Chapter 2)
	To discuss familiar story themes and link to their own experience, e.g. illness, getting lost, going away	Children liken aspects of Gerda's display of loyalty and friendship to their own experiences (Chapter 5)
Y3	To identify and discuss main and recurring characters. Evaluate their behaviour and justify views	Children hot-seat the Hunter (Chapter 2) and discuss what they have learned about him after the interrogation
Y4	To identify ... the dilemmas faced by characters ... and discuss how the characters deal with them	Children discuss, with the teacher and then in groups, how the new story of the Forest Child might end before preparing their short plays
Y5	To investigate narrative viewpoint and the treatment of different characters, e.g. heroes, villains, and perspectives on action of different characters	Children are presented with the more sympathetic portrayal of the Hunter when they hot-seat him.

You need not be strait-jacketed by such objectives, of course, or by those offered in similar publications – the mapping of the story is quite an appropriate activity for children beyond Year 2, for example – but they remind us of the breadth of experience children are entitled to and indicate when they should be ready to engage with particular challenges. Here, for example, there is a clear suggestion that children should be able to cope with the problematical perspective of the Hunter by Year 5.

The reading and scripting of playtext is another area of overlap between English and drama. In the very early years, children's learning to chant repetitive phrases as they occur in nursery rhymes and at the end of stories such as *Little Red Riding Hood*, where they can join in as either the girl or the wolf, can introduce them to the principles of sequenced dialogue. Play reading can become an enjoyable part of guided or group reading periods, with children being encouraged to play with dynamics and tone of voice in order to convey simple characterisation rather than simply to decode the phonics. In the junior years, children should read such texts with increased fluency and independence and occasionally be encouraged to perform them, with script, to the rest of the class. The conventions used for writing script can move from the cartoon use of speech bubbles to collaborative group play-writing by the end of Year 2. These scripts can be short and based upon scenes from stories the children know or have been working on in drama and role-play. By the end of Year 5, children should be able to write using the conventional layout of playscript and might choose to present aspects of their story writing in this form when suitable. You might encourage children to write the kind of stage directions which give clues as to how the characters should speak their lines, with phrases such as (*whispering*) or (*shouting in anger*) being included when apposite. Again, detailed guidance for the development of children's ability to read and write playscripts is offered in the National Literacy Strategy.

The important point when using objectives from other curriculum areas to help plan for progression in drama, whether in PSE or in English, is to maintain a symbiotic relationship between the two areas. As was pointed out in Chapter 4, neither area should simply service the other; both should benefit equally from the connection. But there remain those elements of drama to address which distinguish it from other areas of the curriculum and which cannot therefore be mapped elsewhere. For example, important as the reading and writing activities described above are to children's introduction to the encoding and decoding of conventional drama, the actual realisation of a text for performance purposes is a complex process which moves into cognitive territories beyond the acquisition of literacy. For, despite its natural eclecticism, the parameters of drama stretch beyond speaking, listening, reading playtexts, working with stories and cooperating in groups. It is to what makes drama distinctive that we now turn.

Making, performing and responding

In the introduction, we emphasised that drama is a narrative art form that makes symbolic use of real time, real space, real objects and real people in order to fashion its meanings. As with all art, these meanings are shaped into a form in order to be communicated. The Arts Council of Great Britain's 1992 publication *Drama in Schools* separated this process into three areas of attainment: Making, Performing and Responding. This is the most recent national guidance available for UK schools and the terminology it provides constitutes as valid a starting point as any for considering progression in drama. Some exemplification is needed, however, if we are to use it to plot progression, as these categories are not always as clearly separable as at first might appear.

Crudely speaking, we may define *making* as the crafting or creation of a piece of theatre, *performing* as the presentation of this creation and *responding* as the process of bearing active witness to it. It is a model which fits easily alongside the examples of performance drama discussed in the previous chapter but in the participatory and improvisatory forms which often characterise classroom drama, the distinctions may not be so clear-cut. For, within the kind of whole-class drama described in Chapters 3 and 4, children will sometimes perform *as* they make and their responses might best be gauged as participants within the action rather than as observers outside it. In the Saxon drama, for example, the making and performing of the ritual are clear enough but children will respond to it as participants *in* it as much as witnesses *to* it. Later, when the teacher in role as traveller arrives with news of the approach of the Vikings, an appropriate response from a child will be to react in role rather than to reflect out of role. Such a blurring of the boundaries can be characteristic of the 'lived through' experience of this kind of improvised, participatory drama suitable for children throughout the primary years. Nevertheless, it is important that, as they mature, children are given increased opportunities to work more or less distinctively within the three areas and to reflect upon the processes they involve.

- *Making* will encourage them to investigate and articulate issues of dramatic form.
- *Performing* will add to this a consideration of dramatic skills.
- *Responding* will encourage children to consider what they think and feel about a drama as a whole, stimulating them into a reflection and analysis of what actually constitutes good drama.

Such objectives will indeed require children to be given the time and the means to craft and critically reflect upon aspects of their work with a measure of independence in the upper junior years. Their ability to take advantage of such opportunities will, however, depend to a large extent upon the quality of their previous experiences of drama.

Learning objectives specific to drama

The publication *Drama in Schools* offers a short list of end of Key Stage Statements classified under the three headings *Making, Performing and*

Responding as a guide to progression in the drama curriculum. They are, however, narrowly geared towards play-making and performance with the result that the targets for children at the end of Year 2, in particular, fail to accommodate the variety of drama work suitable for young children. This perhaps indicates that the distinction between Making, Performing and Responding is unhelpful for early years teachers and that more general statements are required. Below we present an alternative set of end of Key Stage Statements which, we hope, are clear and challenging, flexible enough to cover all aspects of the drama curriculum and which recognise that, for children in the early years, attainment targets for drama and those for personal, social and moral education will often converge. In doing this, we have drawn heavily from the 1989 HMI publication *Drama from 5 to 16*:

By the end of Year 2, children should be able to:

- play inventively and with concentration, both on their own and with others;
- understand and take pleasure in the difference between the conventions of dramatic play and the normal social conventions of the classroom;
- identify with characters and actions through role-playing, for instance in a dramatised story, and as spectators of a live performance;
- have the confidence and ability to put across a particular point of view;
- realise that the views of individuals do not always coincide;
- learn how to work together to solve human and practical problems;
- explore the differences between right and wrong in simple dilemmas posed through drama;
- make use of some simple performance conventions e.g. mime, movement, stillness;
- discuss why they think a performance is good with reference to plot, character, use of voice and gesture and, where applicable, use of costume, setting, lighting etc.;
- actively take part in short, whole-class performance projects.

A set of learning objectives, or end of Key Stage Statements, for Key Stage 2 could include the following:

Making

By the end of Year 6 children should be able to:

- invent and develop roles in specific situations;
- help create classroom dramas which explore particular issues with a practical, social or moral dimension;

- shape dramatic space and position bodies and objects meaningfully within it;
- sequence material for dramatic purposes, such as, for example, the clear presentation of a narrative;
- make symbolic use of objects, materials, light and sound;
- script simple dramatic scenes, making appropriate use of format, stage directions etc.

Performing

By the end of Year 6 children should be able to:

- use movement, voice and gesture in a controlled manner in order to convey meaning;
- sustain, in role or in performance, an intended atmosphere (such as humour) or an intended emotion (such as fear or anger);
- interpret appropriate playscripts for performance purposes.

Responding

By the end of Year 6 children should:

- have been given opportunities to discuss drama and performance from a range of sources and cultures, including classroom drama, live performance (including Theatre in Education programmes), TV and film drama;
- be able to recognise good work in drama through a critical observation of the characters created, the issues involved, the processes employed and the skills demonstrated.

Policy and practice

In addition to such objectives, a framework for progression will need to show how the principles of offering children increased complexity, control, depth and independence within their drama work can be put into practice. This can be done by organising examples of children's progress throughout the primary years under the following three statements of policy:

1. Children should be given increased opportunities to take responsibility for their drama work.

2. The challenges, in terms of both form and content, should become increasingly complex.
3. Both drama as a subject, and children's individual achievements within it, should become increasingly visible as children move up the school.

However, when attempting to turn these policy statements into practice, you will need to bear the following points in mind:

- The extent to which older primary school children will be able to meet responsibility and challenge will depend upon contextual factors, including their overall personal and social development; their previous experience of drama; and whether they are used to being given such opportunities in other curriculum areas.
- Throughout the primary years, the teacher will always be needed to provide a framework, focus and strong direction to children's drama. Giving children increased responsibility changes the nature of your input: it doesn't diminish it. For example, you will retain the responsibility for ensuring that the production values of any public performance work remain very high. Statements such as 'it was all the children's own work' cannot become a substitute for a teacher's accountability.
- The implication that drama as a subject should become more visible in the upper primary school does not mean that it shouldn't be given independent timetabling in earlier years. Nor does it imply that cross-curricular drama work as described in Chapter 4 should then cease. It is simply to indicate that, as children's knowledge, skills and understanding grow, they need the space to explore in greater depth if they are to continue to make the progress of which they are capable. We do suggest, however, that primary schools with drama specialists working in the lower school give careful consideration as to how they might be deployed to advise or assist with the teaching of drama in the upper school.
- As we emphasised in Chapter 2, you need to plan for learning outcomes which are visible and therefore more or less capable of being assessed.

Below we offer some guidelines as to how each of the three statements of policy might look in practice. Some examples are given and, where they are not provided, we invite you to find further examples from previous chapters. The list is self-evidently *not* exhaustive and is intended to inform your school's policy on progression, not to offer a blueprint for it.

Children should be given increased opportunities to take responsibility for their drama work

When	By the end of Year 2	By the end of Year 6
the teacher guides the drama	she will use teacher in role extensively to provide and maintain the focus and to provoke reaction among the children (e.g. the Teddy drama, Chapter 3)	she will use teacher in role more sparingly and with more variety of purpose, e.g. to change focus (Saxon drama, Chapter 4) or to challenge opinions (as the 'nice' Hunter, Chapter 2). She will be active in setting up frameworks for the drama but often stay outside the action (e.g. Trojan drama, Chapter 4)
the whole class is in role	children will usually role-play homogeneous groups, sharing similar perspectives with one another (e.g. the toys in the Teddy drama; the staff helping the old lady in the café drama, Chapter 3); they tend to follow and be reactive to the teacher in role	they can consider and construct roles and characters specific to particular contexts, often with conflicting views they are able clearly to distance themselves from their actions in and out of role; they can be more proactive and individualised in whole-class drama
initially acting out a story	the teacher will control the process, for example by using a 'story stick'; children should involve themselves willingly and await their turn	children can sequence the tale themselves in note form. They can act it out spontaneously in groups, with one child taking on the role of narrator

sequencing material	the teacher can invite the children to think why something has happened in a drama, or to consider what might happen next	at a given moment of crisis, children can discuss the possible outcomes and choose the direction the drama should take (e.g. Saxon drama); children can decide how movement work devised by groups should be sequenced for presentation
writing scripts	the teacher can write down and use phrases suggested by children for a sound collage (e.g. The Snow Queen); children can write collaboratively in groups, using different colours to indicate different characters	subject to the teacher's monitoring and advice, children should take responsibility for scripting sections of a class performance. These should be crafted carefully, redrafted and should include detailed stage directions
working from scripts	children should enjoy the group reading of play-scripts as part of their structured reading scheme. They can mime appropriate actions and add simple sound effects	children can physicalise the environment suggested by a text in a given space, interpret and convey mood and differentiate character types through voice and gesture
using space	children should be sensitive to the positioning and grouping of others. They should be able to work in groups in a given space without intruding into the space of other groups	the teacher can ask children to set up the space and organise the actors within it to represent a specific place, e.g. the Enchanter's room
using objects and materials symbolically	children should be actively responsive to the teacher's use of an object, e.g. a hat, a teddy	children can use cloth to create their own images representing, e.g., the Enchanter's Daughter's sense of entrapment

The challenges, both in terms of form and content, should become increasingly complex

When	By the end of Year 2	By the end of Year 6
exploring moral issues	children should be encouraged to articulate, either in or out of role, the differences between right and wrong; children can be given roles as active moral agents, e.g. helpers, rescuers	children should engage with problems where issues of who is right and wrong are not clear-cut; children can examine alternative courses of action both inside and outside the drama
choosing stories for drama	the teacher should look for stories where characters are 'types' (e.g. heroes, villains, tricksters) and where the narrative offers security (e.g. *Jack and the Beanstalk* and *The Snow Queen* where evil is defeated)	the teacher might choose a story where the issues and characters are more complex and where conventional narrative structures are confounded (e.g. *I'll Take You to Mrs Cole*, where the threat of evil is seen to be illusory; or *The Enchanter's Daughter*, where traditional fairy tale values are subtly inverted)
structuring drama	the teacher will generally organise material to follow or explore a linear narrative	the teacher can begin to employ more complex narrative structures, e.g. **flashback, parallel scenes**
using gesture	children should be able to create and hold still images to depict clear moments of action	children can explore how different gestures and altered body language can change relationships within the same social situation
working in movement	children can move freely and expressively to simple stimuli; they can develop simple motifs and respond to choreography	children can devise, refine, rehearse and perform more complex, clearly expressive movement motifs

taking part in a production	all children can enjoy being part of a spectacle within the security of whole-group activities	individual children should have the opportunity to share in the responsibility for particular areas in which they are skilled and interested, e.g. scripting, singing, acting, providing musical accompaniment, programme design, lighting, etc.

Both drama as a subject, and children's individual achievements within it, should become increasingly visible as children move up the school

When	By the end of Year 2	By the end of Year 6
planning a sequence of lessons	drama is likely to be integrated into other curriculum areas with limited discrete objectives	drama will link with other curriculum areas but with more pronounced, discrete objectives
assessing	assessment criteria will be largely cross-curricular	assessment criteria should be more drama-specific
reporting	specific comments for drama are likely to be included within other curriculum areas	where schools report on all curriculum subjects, drama could be given its own section on a child's report form

If you find the above framework helpful, you might adapt it to apply to the drama-related programmes of study in your own school. To expand upon it, you could add additional columns for Reception and Year 4 children, and include more categories for exemplification.

In 1999, the QCA published a framework for progression in drama activities as an appendix to its document *Teaching Speaking and Listening at Key Stages 1 and 2*. It suggests specific activities and teaching objectives more prescriptive than the guidance we offer here and its idea of a drama curriculum ties it very closely to the *National Curriculum for English* and the *National Literacy Strategy*. It does, however, loosely correspond to the Making, Performing and Responding framework for drama and you may well find its references to specific tasks a useful complement to the framework we offer here. The guidance is enclosed in full as Appendix 3.

Assessing, recording and reporting on progression

The same features of drama which make issues of progression difficult also problematise the field of assessment. The communal nature of drama means that it is in groups rather than as individuals that the children produce work; the temporal nature of drama means that, unlike a piece of writing or a painting, the qualities in what the children produce are, by their very nature, impermanent and therefore easy for you as teacher to forget. Furthermore, there may be teachers in your school who wish to regard drama as an assessment-free zone, valuing it exclusively for the enjoyment and motivation it engenders. However, the brief comments on pages 101–3 are indicative of the fact that issues of progression, the assessment of progression, and the recording and reporting of progression are inextricably interrelated. If we accept the need for progression then some method for charting and reporting upon progression is an inevitable consequence.

Primary school teachers have become increasingly conversant with issues of Assessment, Recording and Reporting (AR&R) over recent years with the result that most schools now have in place agreed policies and practices within this area. Any system of AR and R that you adopt for drama must, of necessity:

- fit within your school's existing practices;
- be economical in terms of your time and energy;
- fit with why and how your school values drama;
- fit with how your school positions drama within the curriculum.

The guidelines for progression offered in this chapter would suggest that, up to the end of Year 2, children's drama work could adequately be assessed and reported on within a cross-curricular framework, provided that the significance of its learning objectives is recognised and space is made for them to be developed. It is likely that in many primary schools this will continue throughout Key Stage 2. They may choose to use documentation in subjects such as English to help map out a child's progression in drama, and choose to assess, record and hence report those aspects of it within those curriculum areas. On the other hand, if specialist provision is available, or if a school adopts the end of Key Stage Statements offered here, it may be more straightforward to assess and report on drama discretely, at least within the upper primary years. In the final analysis, what matters is that:

- an agreed and thorough map of progression exists;
- teachers are clear what their objectives are;
- these objectives are adaptable to suit the needs of particular groups of children; and

- recorded and reported information exists in some valid and systematic form.

Perhaps the most difficult principle of good practice in AR and R is the need for the teacher to base her judgements on visible achievement. Statements such as 'Sunjay has grown in confidence' do not mean much unless they are backed by concrete examples such as 'He readily agreed to be one of the narrators in our class assembly' or 'He has taken on some demanding roles and spoke out confidently in role as the pharaoh in our Egyptian drama'. You can find such visible evidence of learning from a variety of sources, some within drama lessons, some from related work in other curriculum areas. A few of these sources, with advice as to what assessment-related information you might find in them, are offered below.

Child's activity observed and noted

If you teach in the early years, you might ask a member of the support staff to observe children in the play corner and note aspects of their play which you specify in advance. Teachers in any of the primary years might regularly track three or four different children during each drama session, making brief notes against the specific learning outcomes noted in their lesson plans. When any child produces work which is particularly striking, this, too, can be quickly noted. Such quick assessments can focus and capture judgements on individual children without distracting you from the class or the drama as a whole. These comments could focus particularly on objectives related to the making of drama as the use of video and photography (see below) can help you assess performance work.

Video and sound recordings

These might include:

- recordings of small classroom presentations;
- recordings of work in progress for a school production;
- the school production itself; or
- an audio recording of sound collages created by groups during a drama lesson.

They can be used to inform children's own self-evaluations and can constitute a permanent record of individual children's achievements in performing drama at a given moment in time.

Photographs

These, too, can constitute a permanent record, capturing still images of individual children's use of space and gesture and can also contribute to a classroom wall display.

Writing in or out of role

Children's writing can be particularly helpful when assessing their responses to and understanding of the content of a drama. It might consist of one or two sentences of emergent writing from a child in Reception and can take a variety of forms for older children – a scripted scene or dialogue; a detailed description of a significant moment; a letter to or by one of the characters or an entry from one of their diaries; a piece of story writing, etc. It will be less work for you, of course, if such writing is planned as an integral part of children's language work and is not tacked-on as an additional activity for assessment purposes only.

Drawings and art work

These can range from a child's imaginative response to a place or a character within a drama to a carefully crafted mask, piece of costume or prop to be used in a performance.

Brief self-evaluation profiles

Suitable for older children at the end of a drama project, you can use these to solicit children's comments against specific questions or criteria to help inform your overall assessment.

For assessment to be manageable in primary drama, it must not become over-complex and the methods adopted must, in the end, make your reporting of attainment easier, more specific and more accurate. There is no need for your dramas to become narrowly assessment driven, nor for AR and R to spoil the satisfaction many children derive from drama, regardless of their individual levels of attainment. In the final analysis, if children achieve and make progress in a subject and understand how and why they have done so, the motivation this engenders in their work adds to rather than detracts from their sense of enjoyment. Your day-to-day assessment in action will almost certainly follow these principles – informing children what is good in their work, telling them why it is good, and letting them know how they can do it better. When you have a sound understanding of progression, of what it means to get better at drama, the feedback you give to the children can only be of benefit to your teaching and their learning.

Publications referred to in this chapter

Arts Council of Great Britain (1992) *Drama in Schools*. London: ACGB.

Citizenship Foundation (1994) *You, Me, Us: Social and Moral Responsibility for Primary Schools*. London: Citizenship Foundation.

Department for Education and Employment (1998) *The National Literacy Strategy: Framework for Teaching*. London: DfEE.

Department for Education and Employment (1999) *The National Curriculum: A Handbook for Teachers*. London: DfEE, QCA.

Her Majesty's Inspectorate (1989) *Drama from 5 to 16*. London: HMSO.

National Curriculum Council (1990) *The Arts 5–16: A Curriculum Framework*. Harlow: Oliver and Boyd.

QCA (1999a) *Early Learning Goals*. London: QCA, DfEE.

QCA (1999b) *Teaching Speaking and Listening in Key Stages 1 and 2*. London: QCA.

SCAA (1994) *Model Syllabuses for Religious Education*. London: SCAA.

Appendix 1

The Forest Child

The Forest Child, written by Richard Edwards and illustrated by Peter Malone, is published by Orion Children's Books, London.

The text of the story is printed below with the permission of the publishers.

We strongly recommend that teachers buy this beautifully illustrated book for their classroom.

There was once a child who was raised by the animals of the forest. The Wolf taught her to run. The Bear taught her to find food. The Beaver taught her to swim.

She ran silently over the forest floor. She knew where to find honey and the juiciest berries. She dived in the lake behind the beaver dam.

One day a Hunter came to the forest, bringing with him a boy from the village to carry his traps and snares. 'Stay here and don't move till I get back!' said the Hunter. But the boy got bored sitting still. He walked between the trees, where the light was dim. It was like being under water in a green sea. At the edge of the clearing, the boy from the village met the Forest Child. She backed away, growling like a wolf. 'Who are you?' called the boy. 'Don't be afraid.' But the girl turned and ran off into the shadows.

Each day that followed, the boy returned to the clearing, hoping to meet the Forest Child again. At last she lost all fear of him, and they would walk together along twisting paths in the forest's secret heart. One day, the Hunter was out checking his traps and saw the children passing. He followed them back to the clearing. When the boy had left for home, the Hunter burst from his hiding place and grabbed the Forest Child. 'Caught you, little bird!' he snarled. The Hunter took the wild girl to the village. She fought and bit and twisted and kicked, but the Hunter was too strong for her. He locked her up.

The Hunter decided to teach the girl how to behave. He gave her a cup to drink from and a spoon to eat with, but she didn't know what they were for. The girl would not speak, so the Hunter laid a sheet of paper on the table. 'Here, write your name,' he said, giving her a pen. The girl looked at the pen and turned it over in her hand. She didn't understand what she was supposed to do. 'What's the matter with you?' shouted the Hunter. The girl's eyes glittered with tears. She wanted to go back to the forest. 'WRITE YOUR NAME!' The girl stood up. She broke the pen in pieces and threw them at the Hunter, spattering him with ink. 'You stupid girl!' he yelled, raising his arm. Just then the village boy hammered on the door. 'Don't shout at her,' he said. 'She doesn't understand.' 'She'd better understand soon,' said the Hunter, 'or there'll be trouble! And there'll be trouble for you too, if you don't mind your own business!' He slammed the door. The boy hesitated for a moment, and then turned towards the forest.

The animals of the forest missed the girl they had raised. All day they ran between the tall trees, searching. They found her scent on the ground and followed it to the clearing, where it mixed with other scents. The Wolf howled.

On the outskirts of the village the animals met the boy coming to find them. 'Quick! This way!' The animals leapt in through the windows. They chased the Hunter round the room, out into the darkness and across the fields. The Wolf bit a hole in the Hunter's trousers, the Beaver tripped him, and the Bear sent him rolling down a hill, right into the middle of a big mud puddle. The Hunter sank from sight.

The sun streams down like gold between the trees. The girl and the village boy run silently over the forest floor. She teaches him to find honey and the juiciest berries. They swim and dive in the lake behind the beaver dam.

They all sleep together in a jumbled heap, under a million stars.

Appendix 2

A selection of drama conventions

The list below contains a number of conventions or strategies to help you structure your drama work. Most of them have been referred to in the chapters of this book. For further examples and guidance, see *Structuring Drama Work* by Jonothan Neelands (details in bibliography).

Alter-ego/ voices in the head	The class or group is asked to think about the conflicting voices in the minds of characters faced with difficult situations or decisions. The class may be divided into groups so that the voices in the head of more than one character can be explored simultaneously.
Captions	These might be slogans, titles, inscriptions, etc., which accompany what is presented visually. They might be written down but are more likely to be spoken aloud to accompany the images.
Collective role	The role of a character is played by more than one child simultaneously. Each child might express a different aspect of the character's personality.
Conscience alley	The class are formed into two lines between which a character can walk. As she walks down the 'alley' the lines form and her thoughts are spoken by the rest of the class. She may be on the way to some event in the drama or she may be faced with making a difficult decision.
Flashback	A common technique in film. The present action or story line is temporarily suspended and children are asked to devise a scene from the past that might explain a character's current behaviour or situation.
Formal meeting (meeting in role)	The whole class is in role as a group that needs to meet to hear news, report on progress or make decisions. The teacher may or may not be in role with the class, depending on whether she needs to influence the direction the meeting takes.

Forum theatre	Individual members of the class are chosen to enact a particular scene. The rest of the class observe, but both actors and observers can stop the action at any point to ask for or give guidance as to how the scene might be developed.
Hot-seating	Someone (either teacher or child) assumes a role and is questioned by the rest of the group. The role may be signalled by sitting in a particular seat (the 'hot seat') or perhaps by wearing an item of costume or holding a particular artefact.
Mantle of the expert	The class take on roles which have specialist knowledge or expertise that is needed within the drama. In the 'reservoir' drama in Chapter 4, for instance, the roles adopted by the children are more knowledgeable than the role adopted by the teacher.
Maps/diagrams	These can be used to provide additional information about the context and setting for the drama. They can be drawn collectively so that everyone gets the chance to influence the eventual outcome.
Mime	This can range from 'moving like the toys' as in the drama in Chapter 3, to more carefully crafted and symbolic uses of movement and gesture. It may be accompanied and supported by teacher narration.
Narration	The teacher may use narration to introduce, link or conclude action. It might be used to slow and intensify action such as 'the animals crept slowly towards the Hunter's cottage'; to mark the passage of time as in 'the next night the animals met again'; or to introduce the next stage such as 'each year the people of the village would gather to celebrate the harvest'.
Overheard conversations	The class might be invited to 'overhear' a conversation or part-conversation which sheds some light on the situation in the drama but also adds further tension.
Parallel Scenes	Two or more scenes which in reality would happen in different places and/or at different times are played next to each other. The action of one scene can be 'frozen' and the other brought alive to explore the connections and tensions between them.
Ritual (or ceremony)	The class devise ways of marking events that are significant to the people in the drama, drawing on their existing knowledge and experience. They may include music, movement, dance, spoken language, special food, etc.

Role on the wall/floor	A role is represented in picture form. Information about the person concerned can be added as the drama progresses and we learn more about them.
Short play	Exactly what it says! This is best kept very short but it provides children with the opportunity to present a coherent story line using many elements of drama simultaneously – movement, dialogue, objects, perhaps a scene change or two.
Sound collage	Sounds are made, often by the whole class using voice, body and/or instruments, either to accompany actions or to create atmosphere.
Still image/ tableau	Groups work to create an image of a moment in time using their own bodies. Often it will represent people 'frozen' in the middle of some action (as in the Saxon drama in Chapter 4) but it may represent a more abstract idea such as bravery (as in the Trojan drama).
Teacher in role	The teacher takes a full part in the drama, often using her role to manage the drama from within the action. Teacher roles can have a variety of statuses offering different power relationships within the group, as explored in Chapter 4.
Telephone conversations	Sometimes these are devised in pairs to explore the way information is given or news is broken. The teacher may also speak just one half of a conversation, creating tension and challenging the class to infer what is said on the other end of the line.
Thought tracking	The private thoughts or reactions of a character are spoken publicly, either by the character himself or by other participants in the drama. It might be used when the action is frozen or used in conjunction with still images.

Appendix 3

QCA Guidelines for Progression Years 1 to 6

DRAMA ACTIVITIES	FOCUS ON TEACHING	EXTENDING AND REINFORCING
Y1T1 **improvisation** • explore familiar themes and characters • respond to 'teacher in role' to explore character • respond in role to create stories	extended role-play • allocate different roles, include the teacher and children • notice how people in different roles behave differently	• reinforce differences in roles in home corner and role-play
T2 **performance and improvisation** • act out own stories and well-known stories to different audiences, eg *peers, other classes* • respond as themselves in a fictional setting to create stories	using puppets • use different ways of speaking and acting for different characters • make a play and perform it for others	in reading aloud • use different voices for characters
T3 **responding to drama** • consider motives and issues in response to others' performance, eg *in visiting theatre groups* • consider character, motive and story development by reflecting on own drama	discussing why a performance is good • consider dramatic moments of plot, character, special effects and audience participation	make evaluations after dance, role-play, listening to reports and comments
Y2T1 **improvisation** • adopt appropriate roles in small or large groups • use texts, materials, artefacts, images and objects as stimulus • consider alternative courses of action from those in stories or plays	building on the plot and character of a story • improvise an ending • compare this with the writer's version	• use improvisation as a way of responding and interpreting in different subjects
T2 **responding to drama** • consider aspects of stagecraft in a live or recorded performance • consider other elements of performance that create mood and atmosphere	comparing two short video extracts • choose words to describe costume, setting, lighting etc. • identify atmosphere	• notice presentation in a range of TV and video programmes
T3 **performance** • present parts of traditional and own stories to peers • present work from different areas of the curriculum to others	comparing the presentation of investigation into a subject with the dramatisation of a story • consider the range of techniques of presenting • consider different languages for different purposes • consider interest and intelligibility to the listener	• present information and story dramatisation
Y3T1 **writing and performance of drama** • present drama for other audiences • sequence and develop events and characters	writing and performing the script for a play in groups • plan characters and events before writing dialogue • use different ways to engage the interest of the intended audience	• identify differences between prose and playscript • consider dialogue, stage directions, layout
T2 **improvisation and role-play** • use drama to explore key moments from a text • respond in role, using language appropriate to given context • consider starting points, finishing points and key moments in dramatic stories	during the reading of a story • identify turning points and use tableau or freeze frame to highlight and develop these moments • develop character through language	• use role-play to explore moral and social issues

	DRAMA ACTIVITIES	FOCUS ON TEACHING	EXTENDING AND REINFORCING
T3	**responding to drama** • focus on themes and characters in live and/or recorded performances • identify and discuss qualities in others' performances	after watching a play • gather information on characters from dialogue, gesture, action, costume, relationships to others • consider how well characters were portrayed	• consider non-verbal aspects of communication and their impact, e.g. *eye contact, movement, posture*
Y4T1	**improvisation and role-play** • interpret a range of stimulus material • explore situations described in factual documents • recognise how the roles in situations can be approached from different viewpoints	improvisation based on a selection of objects, e.g. *letters, photographs, clothing* • improvise a scene in which characters have distinct roles and different views of the objects	• use improvisation to explore and enact moments in history, based on source material
T2	**writing and performing drama** • develop scripts based on improvisation • compare the performance of improvisation and scripted drama	improvising and scripting scenes developed from a novel • perform scripted scenes • consider differences for actors when improvising or delivering a script	• compare dialogue in novels and stories, in performances, and face to face
T3	**responding to drama** • discuss the effectiveness of communication in own and others' work • compare different live and/or recorded performances • accept the response and feedback of others	watching performances of the same script by different groups • discuss effects and how they were achieved • compare different groups' emphases and strengths	• develop vocabulary for discussing performance and feedback on talk, e.g. *upstaging, dominant, realistic, convincing*
Y5T1	**writing and performing drama** • develop scenes or incidents from novels or poems • write a play/script based on a scene in a novel or poem, or on a further episode, and present it	developing and improvising scenes from a novel • perform scripted scenes • compare with the original scene in the novel	• consider how drama scripts are organised and laid out, including descriptions of sets and stage directions
T2	**improvisation and role-play** • explore different ways of life in other cultures or periods of history • work in and out of role	a role-play based on issues and events on which people have strong views, e.g. *child labour in Victorian England and nowadays* • invite children in role to give views • improvise discussion by key players • discuss how arguments were presented and whose views might change	• note how people's views are influenced by their past experiences
T3	**responding to drama** • recognise theatrical effects, e.g. *sound and silence, movement and stillness, tempo* • describe and discuss style and genre in performances seen	enacting a ceremony, e.g. *a coronation or wedding, using speech and silence* • consider how meaning and impact are expressed by movement, gesture, etc. • mime scenes, focusing on how to convey meaning without words	• consider different ways to convey emotions such as humour and sadness
Y6T1	**responding to drama** • consider the overall impact of a live or recorded performance • recall and describe the drama/theatre forms used by others • discuss alternative presentations of the performance	watching a complete performance (live or taped) of a classic adaptation • identify dramatic ways of conveying characters and ideas, and building tension • consider differences between performed and written versions	• adapt scenes from classic texts for different audiences, e.g. *younger children*
T2	**improvisation and role-play** • present poems aloud • explore themes involving dreams, hopes, fears and expectations	presenting poems using narrator, chorus, different voices, tableaux • discuss the relationship of presentation to response to poem • consider the effectiveness of presentation	• use different voice techniques when reading aloud, presenting information, giving instructions
T3	**writing and performing drama** • devise work for a target audience • redraft their own scripts created for performance in the light of feedback	devising a performance for an audience outside school, e.g. *young children, old people* • consider how to adapt the presentation for a specific audience	• read reviews of theatre, TV and live entertainment and discuss the target audience, identifying clues such as reference to topic; actors and special effects

Bibliography

Ten good story books for drama with 4- to 7-year-olds

Janet and Allan Ahlberg, *The Jolly Postman*. Heinemann.
  The story of the postman's round and the letters he delivers, any of which might make a good starting point.

John Burningham, *Oi! Get Off Our Train*. Jonathan Cape.
  A boy dreams of a train on which endangered animals of the world join him on a journey to safety. Drama can be developed by adding other animals who join the journey and deciding whom they might see in order to talk about their problems.

Amy Ehrlich, *The Walker Book of Fairy Tales*. Walker Books.
  Traditional stories such as these are very good sources. For example, *The Elves and the Shoemaker* could be explored by thinking about where the elves go next – who might deserve their help?

Jane Hissey, *Old Bear*. Walker Books
  The story of a bear who gets left in the attic and gets forgotten – another good 'toys come to life' story.

Shirley Hughes, *Dogger*. Bodley Head.
  An early years classic about Dave who loses his beloved Dogger. Lots of opportunities for hot-seating the characters, creating the summer fair and helping Dave to get Dogger back.

Margaret Mahy, *The Man Whose Mother Was a Pirate*. Puffin Books.
  The story of a man and his mother who run away to sea. The drama can centre around where they go, what happens and how they might persuade Mr Fat to run away too.

Juliet and Charles Snape, *Giant*. Walker Books.
  Giant is the mountain on which a village depends. One night she gets up and leaves because she is unhappy about the way the villagers have treated her. The drama can explore the associated environmental issues and the villagers' efforts to persuade her to return.

Susan Varley, *Badger's Parting Gifts*. Andersen Press.
  This story is about the death of Old Badger and the ways in which his friends remember him. There are roles for children as the various animals whom Badger helps when he is alive and opportunities to explore the ways in which he might have been remembered.

Martin Waddell, *When the Teddy Bears Came*. Walker Books.
  A story about teddy bears arriving at a child's house after the birth of his baby sister. Children can take the roles of the teddy bears and talk about why the boy seems unhappy – rather like the drama in Chapter 3.

Martin Waddell, *Owl Babies*. Walker Books.

> The story of three baby owls whose mother leaves them alone for a while. Roles for the children might include other young animals who live in the same forest. The drama might also investigate where their mother went and why.

Ten good story books for drama with 7- to 11-year-olds

Antonia Barber, *The Mousehole Cat*. Walker Books.

> Based on a Cornish legend, this story tells of how Mowzer, the cat, and old Tom the fisherman, brave the storm to save their village. Lots of opportunities for exploring how the story can be retold using sound, light and movement.

Barbara Juster Esbensen, *Ladder to the Sky*. Little Brown.

> The story of how the gift of healing came to the Ojibway nation. This is only one example of Barbara Esbensen's retellings of Native American legends – all of which provide potent material for classroom drama.

Nigel Gray, *I'll Take You to Mrs Cole*. Andersen Press.

> A good story for exploring children's relationships with adults, their fears and their prejudices.

Madhur Jaffrey, *Seasons of Splendour: Tales, Myths and Legends of India*. Puffin Books.

> A splendid collection of stories, many of which provide good sources for drama.

Margaret Mahy, *The Boy With Two Shadows*. Picture Lions.

> A witch asks a boy to look after her shadow while she goes away on holiday, but her shadow behaves badly and causes him some difficulty. Developing the idea that all shadows might have a life of their own opens up the possibility for other shadows to call the witch to account for her behaviour.

Rafe Martin, *Dear as Salt*. Scholastic.

> A retelling of a very ancient tale, this version of the Cinderella story provided the source for Shakespeare's opening scene in *King Lear*. A king tests the love of his three daughters, but is furious with the response of his youngest. The idea of the king having three thrones which he uses according to his moods offers a good starting point – the children can make 'living carvings' that are part of each throne which change and shift as the story develops.

Alice and Martin Provensen, *Shaker Lane*. Walker Books.

> The story of a small rural community which is changed forever by the coming of a reservoir. Lots of possibilities for exploring the impact of such a development on a community in similar ways to the drama described in Chapter 4.

James Reeves, *Heroes and Monsters: Legends of Ancient Greece*. Pan Books.

> This book was the source for the story of the siege of Troy which was used for the drama described in Chapter 4. The stories are well told and provide good sources for storytelling and/or drama.

Martin Waddell, *Coming Home*. Simon and Schuster.

> A boy travels from America with his grandfather to visit his home in Ireland. A story of age, youth and memory.

David Wisniewski, *Rain Player*. Clarion Books.

> The story, based on a Mayan legend, of a young man who challenges a god to a deadly game.

Ten good books about drama 4–11

Davies, G. *Practical Primary Drama*. Heinemann 1983.

> Although written some time ago, this very readable book still contains helpful guidance for student teachers on the practicalities of drama teaching.

Fleming, M. *Starting Drama Teaching*. David Fulton Publishers 1998.

> A book to sit down and read. Wise, thorough and essential reading for the specialist.

Kitson, N. and Spiby, I. *Drama 7–11*. Routledge 1997.

> Aimed at the non-specialist teacher, this book offers a blend of theory and practical examples by reference to the work of three different teachers.

Morgan, N. and Saxton, J. *Teaching Drama: A Mind of Many Wonders*. Hutchinson 1987.

> Very practical advice on the teaching of drama underpinned by clear and thorough theoretical argument. Essential reading for the specialist.

Neelands, J. *Making Sense of Drama*. Heinemann 1984.

> Although this was written before the introduction of the National Curriculum in Britain, it still contains very helpful and practical guidance which can be used and adapted in a variety of ways.

Neelands, J. *Structuring Drama Work*. Cambridge 1991.

> Although this book was mostly aimed at secondary teachers, many of the structures and conventions it describes are very useful in primary work, particularly with older children. You may need to be prepared to adapt and modify ideas to meet the needs of your children.

Readman, G. and Lamont, G. *Drama – A Handbook for Primary Teachers*. BBC Education 1994.

> Gives a good blend of theoretical understanding and practical ideas for all ages. It offers very useful examples of drama lessons in action and is printed in a large, accessible format.

Somers, J. *Drama in the Curriculum*. Cassell 1994.

> A book for primary and secondary teachers, it gives a detailed look at all aspects of teaching drama. The last two chapters on cross-curricular projects are particularly interesting.

Watts, I. *Just a Minute: Ten Short Plays and Activities for your Classroom*. Pembroke 1990.

> An excellent source of playtexts for the junior classroom. Each play is accompanied by a series of suggestions to help children explore it as a performance text.

Woolland, B. *The Teaching of Drama in the Primary School*. Longman 1993.

> This book can appear quite 'dense' to read at first, but it has some very useful chapters, including one on early years and another on developing work for production. There is also a useful section on developing policy for drama.

Index